Quick & Easy

Quick & Easy

bay books

Contents

Introduction

Easy Dinners

After a long day at work, slaving over a hot stove is often the last thing you feel like doing. But, armed with a well-stocked kitchen and the following ideas, you'll have dinner ready in no time.

Quick and Easy offers a selection of evening meals that are quick to prepare, feature a short list of ingredients (readily available from most large supermarkets) and, most importantly, are full of flavour.

This collection has been divided into nine chapters for easy reference. Meals such as pasta, stir-fries and grills are perfect when you have other plans and have to be out of the house in under an hour. When you have a little more time, stews, casseroles, roasts and bakes are designed to cook themselves while you relax with the family. These casseroles and stews can also be prepared in advance (allowing time for their flavours to develop) and refrigerated or frozen into serving size portions to be eaten another night—all you'll need to do is reheat and serve.

Organization is the key to cooking a variety of convenient and tasty workday meals—a pantry well-stocked with staples is a must. 'Pantry staples' are non-perishable products common to many recipes such as flour, tinned tomatoes and dried herbs, and those, that make versatile accompaniments (rice, pasta and couscous). Restock your pantry when these items are getting low (see suggestions on facing page).

Maintaining a good supply of dry and tinned ingredients, oils, herbs and spices is a great start, but let's not forget to replenish the refrigerator with fresh produce—vegetables, dairy products, meat, poultry and seafood. These products have a comparatively short shelf life and must be restocked more often than pantry staples. Fresh ingredients are essential in making up a balanced meal.

Now that the pantry is full and there is a constant supply of fresh ingredients, the weekday cook has the flexibility to plan in advance for the week's meals or to decide on the spur of the moment what's on tonight's dinner menu.

PANTRY STAPLE INGREDIENTS

- beans, tinned
- breadcrumbs, dry
- capers
- coconut milk
- couscous
- curry pastes
- flour, plain (all-purpose)
- flour, self-raising
- Italian tomato passata, bottled
- mustard (Dijon, wholegrain)
- noodles
- nuts
- oil—it is a good idea to have two types of oil in your pantry at all times; olive oil is good for Mediterranean cooking and salad dressings, while a good all-purpose vegetable or seed oil such as sunflower oil is suitable for general cooking purposes and more compatible to Asian flavours than the distinct flavour of olive oil.
- oyster sauce
- pasta
- polenta (cornmeal)
- rice
- salmon, tinned
- soy sauce
- spices
- stock (in tetra packs)
- sugar, caster (super fine)
- sugar, soft brown
- sweet chilli sauce
- tomato paste (concentrated purée)
- tomatoes, canned
- tuna, canned
- vinegars (balsamic, red wine, white wine, herb infused)

STORAGE

When stored well, packet ingredients should last until their use-by date. Once you have opened packages, remember to seal them properly or store the contents in well-labelled airtight containers.

Check the labels after opening jars of sauces and condiments to ensure they don't require refrigeration after opening. To store pastes (such as tomato and curry) for longer periods of time in convenient small portions, spoon into ice-cube trays, freeze, divide into plastic bags and keep in the freezer until ready to use.

TIME-SAVING TIPS

- Find a good local butcher who pre-dices and slices high-quality meat cuts. This saves not only time but also paying for fat and sinew that you will discard anyway (although take care as some pre-cut meat can be fatty and not at its peak).
- It is handy to have a ready supply of ingredients that are the flavour base for a vast range of meals, in particular garlic, onions, ginger and chillies. Whenever possible, using fresh varieties of these are best as their flavour is far superior to the bottled versions.
- Stocks are a common liquid base to many dishes and, for optimum flavour, it is often recommended to make your own. Good-quality liquid stocks, however, can be purchased and are available in tetra packs or in tins. Tinned stocks are available from Asian stores or in the Asian section of most large supermarkets.
- Leftover bread can be made into breadcrumbs—process pieces of bread in a food processor. Store the crumbs in plastic bags in the freezer, ready for use.
- Plan ahead: read through your recipe and get out all the equipment and ingredients that you need, before you start.
- Decide on any side dishes or accompaniments you wish to serve, and where possible, prepare them while cooking the main meal. Many dishes such as stir-fries, curries and pan-fries are accompanied by rice, which takes about 15 minutes to cook. To maximize time usage, start cooking the rice before you start preparing the rest of your meal.

Soups

CREAMY MUSHROOM SOUP

25 g (1 oz) butter
1 garlic clove, crushed
1 small leek, chopped
2 tablespoons fresh flat-leaf (Italian) parsley, chopped
750 ml (26 fl oz/3 cups) chicken or vegetable stock
400 g (14 oz) Swiss brown mushrooms, sliced
200 ml (7 fl oz) cream
chopped fresh flat-leaf (Italian) parsley, extra, to garnish

Melt the butter in a large saucepan. Add the garlic, leek and parsley and sauté for 2–3 minutes, or until softened. Pour in the stock and bring to the boil. Reduce the heat and simmer for 3 minutes. Add the mushrooms and simmer for a further 5 minutes. Blend the soup in a food processor in batches until smooth. Return to the cleaned pan, pour in the cream and stir until heated through. Season. Serve, garnished with the extra parsley. Serves 4.

Variation: Stir 300 g (10½ oz) thinly sliced chicken breast strips into the stock and cook for 3 minutes before adding the mushrooms.

QUICK MINESTRONE

1 red onion, chopped
150 g (5½ oz) pancetta, finely diced
2 garlic cloves, crushed
1 tablespoon tomato paste (concentrated purée)
1 litre (4 cups) beef stock
300 g (10½ oz) tin cannellini beans, rinsed and drained
250 g (9 oz/1 cup) frozen mixed vegetables
4 tablespoons tubetti or ditalini pasta
shaved Parmesan, to garnish

Cook the onion and pancetta in a large saucepan over medium heat for 2–3 minutes, or until lightly golden. Add the garlic and cook for 1 minute. Stir in the tomato paste to coat the pancetta mixture. Pour in the stock and bring to the boil. Reduce the heat and add the beans, mixed vegetables and pasta. Simmer for 12–15 minutes, or until the pasta is soft. Serve, garnished with the Parmesan. Serves 4.

Note: For a vegetarian alternative, use vegetable stock instead of beef, and add chickpeas or extra mixed vegetables or pulses rather than pancetta.

ORANGE SWEET POTATO, CAPSICUM AND GINGER SOUP

2 red capsicums (peppers), cut into large flat pieces
1 tablespoon olive oil
1 small onion, chopped
2 garlic cloves, chopped
1 tablespoon fresh ginger, grated
¼ teaspoon chilli flakes (optional)
650 g (1 lb 7 oz) orange sweet potato, cut into 2 cm (¾ inch) cubes
750 ml (26 fl oz/3 cups) vegetable stock

Cook the capsicum skin-side-up under a hot grill (broiler) for 10 minutes, or until the skin blackens and blisters. Cool in a plastic bag, then peel and roughly chop. Heat the olive oil in a large saucepan over medium heat. Add the onion and saute for 3–4 minutes, or until softened but not coloured. Add the garlic, ginger and chilli flakes and cook for 1 minute. Add the sweet potato and coat well in the onion mixture. Pour in the stock and 250 ml (9 fl oz/1 cup) water and simmer for 15–20 minutes, or until the sweet potato is soft. Cool slightly and stir in the capsicum. Blend in a food processor in batches until smooth. Season to taste. Delicious served with a dollop of plain yoghurt. Serves 4.

CHINESE BARBECUE PORK AND NOODLE SOUP

1.25 litres (5 cups) chicken stock
3 spring onions (scallions), cut into 4 cm (1½ inch) lengths
4 thin slices fresh ginger
1 tablespoon Chinese rice wine
1 tablespoon oyster sauce
300 g (10½ oz) Chinese barbecue pork fillet, thinly sliced
350 g (12 oz/2 cups) roughly chopped bok choy (pak choy)
200 g (7 oz) fresh flat egg noodles
sliced spring onions (scallions), extra, to garnish

Heat the stock and 250 ml (9 fl oz/1 cup) water in a large saucepan until simmering. Add the spring onion, ginger, rice wine and oyster sauce and simmer for 3–4 minutes. Add the pork and simmer for a further 4–5 minutes, then add the bok choy. Meanwhile, cook the noodles in a saucepan of salted boiling water for 1 minute. Drain and rinse under cold water, then divide among four deep bowls. When the bok choy has just wilted, remove it and the pork with a slotted spoon, and divide among the serving bowls. Cover with the broth and garnish with extra spring onion. Serves 4.

CHUNKY CHICKEN AND VEGETABLE SOUP

Preparation time: 15 minutes
Total cooking time: 15 minutes
Serves 4

1 tablespoon oil
1 carrot, sliced
1 leek, chopped
2 skinless, boneless chicken thighs, cut into 2 cm (¾ inch) pieces
3 tablespoons ditalini pasta
1 litre (4 cups) vegetable stock
2 ripe tomatoes, diced
salt and freshly ground pepper, to season

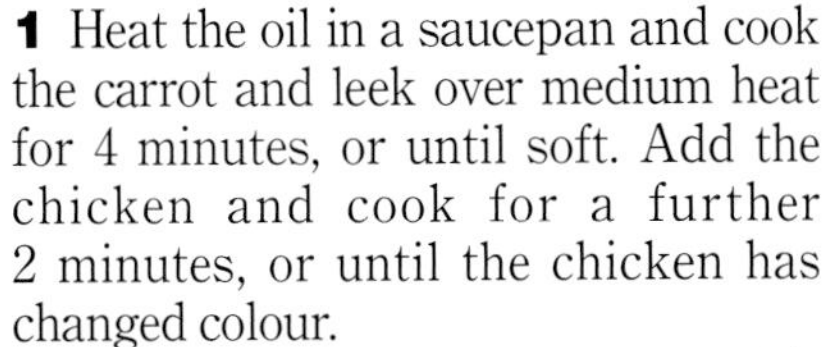

1 Heat the oil in a saucepan and cook the carrot and leek over medium heat for 4 minutes, or until soft. Add the chicken and cook for a further 2 minutes, or until the chicken has changed colour.

2 Add the pasta and the vegetable stock, cover and bring to the boil. Reduce the heat and simmer for 10 minutes, or until the pasta is cooked. Add the tomato halfway through the cooking. Season to taste with salt and freshly ground black pepper. Serve with fresh crusty bread.

COOK'S FILE

Note: Ditalini pasta can be replaced with any small soup pasta.

1

2

CHILLI COCONUT CHICKEN SOUP

Preparation time: 10 minutes
Total cooking time: 10 minutes
Serves 4

3 tablespoons oil
2 cm (¾ inch) piece fresh ginger, peeled and grated
6 spring onions (scallions), sliced into 3 cm (1¼ inch) lengths
6 skinless, boneless chicken breasts, thinly sliced
4 tablespoons sweet chilli sauce
500 ml (17 fl oz/2 cups) coconut milk
2 tablespoons lime juice

1 Heat the oil in a saucepan over high heat, add the ginger and spring onion and cook for 1 minute. Add the chicken and cook for 2–3 minutes, or until golden. Add the sweet chilli sauce and cook for a further 1 minute.

2 Add 350 ml (12 fl oz/1⅓ cups) water and the coconut milk. Bring to the boil, then reduce the heat and simmer for 4–5 minutes. Add the lime juice, season with salt and add a little more sweet chilli sauce, if desired. Serve with lime wedges.

COOK'S FILE

Note: Try adding a little fish sauce at the end of cooking for extra flavour.

1

2

PUMPKIN AND CUMIN SOUP

Preparation time: 10 minutes
Total cooking time: 15 minutes
Serves 4

1 kg (2 lb 4 oz) pumpkin (squash)
500 ml (17 fl oz/2 cups) chicken stock
1 onion, chopped
2 garlic cloves, crushed
2 teaspoons ground cumin
4 tablespoons coconut milk
1 tablespoon lemon juice
chives, chopped, to garnish

1 Peel pumpkin and chop into small chunks. Combine pumpkin in a large saucepan with 250 ml (9 fl oz/1 cup) water, stock, onion, garlic and cumin. Bring to the boil, reduce heat to low and simmer, covered, for 15 minutes or until pumpkin is tender.
2 Transfer mixture, in batches, to food processor or blender and process each batch until smooth. Return mixture to pan. Add coconut milk and lemon juice to pan, stir over medium heat until heated through. Garnish with chopped chives, if desired.

COOK'S FILE

Hint: Pumpkin can be cut into chunks, brushed with oil and baked in the oven until soft.
Variation: If you prefer a thinner consistency, use an extra 250 ml (9 fl oz/1 cup) of stock.

1

2

SPLIT PEA AND HAM SOUP

Preparation time: 10 minutes
Total cooking time: 1–1½ hours
Serves 4–6

250 g (9 oz) green split peas
1.5 litres (6 cups) chicken stock or water
250 g (9 oz) ham off the bone, finely chopped
1 onion, chopped
2 garlic cloves, crushed
½–1 teaspoon dried mixed herbs
4 tablespoons parsley, chopped

1 Place split peas in large pan. Add stock, ham, onion, garlic, herbs and parsley and bring to the boil.
2 Reduce heat to low and simmer, stirring occasionally, for 1–1½ hours or until split peas are soft and pulpy. Garnish with a sprig of flat-leaf (Italian) parsley, if desired.

COOK'S FILE

Hint: Off-cuts of ham are ideal for this recipe. Alternatively, you can use 2–4 rashers thick bacon. Remove the rind and chop roughly.

1

FRENCH ONION SOUP

Preparation time: 5 minutes
Total cooking time: 15–20 minutes
Serves 4

4 large onions
60 g (2¼ oz) butter
1 litre (4 cups) beef stock
8 slices baguette
125 g (4½ oz/½ cup) Cheddar cheese, grated

1 Slice onions thinly. Melt butter in large pan, add onion. Stir constantly oven medium heat for 5–10 minutes or until dark golden, being careful not to burn onion.
Add 250 ml (9 fl oz/1 cup) water, bring to the boil. Reduce heat to low; simmer, covered, for 15 minutes or until onion is very tender. Add stock; bring to the boil. Simmer for 3–5 minutes.
2 Grill (broil) baguette slices on both sides. Top with granted cheese and grill (broil) for another minute or until cheese has melted. Place toast in serving bowls and spoon soup over the top. Serve immediately.

COOK'S FILE

Storage time: Soup can be made up to 3 days in advance. Store, covered, in refrigerator.
Variation: Grilled (broiled) cheese on toast may be served separately if preferred. Grated Gruyére cheese can be used instead of Cheddar.

1

2

3

CORN CHOWDER

Preparation time: 5 minutes
Total cooking time: 25 minutes
Serves 4

1 onion, chopped
2 rashers bacon, chopped
30 g (1 oz) butter
750 g (1 lb 10 oz) potatoes, peeled and cut into small cubes
500 ml (17 fl oz/2 cups) chicken stock
440 g (15½ oz) tin creamed corn
375 ml (13 fl oz/1½ cups) milk

1 Melt butter in large pan, add onion and bacon. Stir over medium heat for 3–5 minutes or until lightly golden. Add potato and stock; bring to the boil. Reduce heat to low and simmer, covered, for 10 minutes.
2 Stir in creamed corn and milk. Simmer, uncovered, stirring occasionally to prevent sticking, for 10 minutes or until potato is tender and chowder has thickened.

COOK'S FILE

Storage time: This recipe can be made up to 3 days before required. Store, covered, in refrigerator.
Hints: Do not allow soup to boil after milk has been added as it may curdle.
For a heartier soup, add 350 g (12 oz) shredded barbecued chicken.

CHICKEN AND SWEET CORN SOUP

Preparation time: 10 minutes
Total cooking time: 20 minutes
Serves 4

- 1 tablespoon oil
- 2 bacon rashers, finely chopped
- 1 small onion, finely chopped
- 2 x 420 g (15 oz) tins creamed corn
- 750 ml (26 fl oz/3 cups) chicken stock
- 2 skinless, boneless chicken thighs, cut into bite-sized pieces
- 2 tablespoons dill, chopped

1 Heat oil in a saucepan and cook bacon and onion over medium heat for 5 minutes, or until onion is soft.
2 Add corn and stock. Bring to the boil, then reduce heat and simmer for 5 minutes. Add chicken and dill and simmer for 5–10 minutes, or until the chicken is cooked through. Season and then serve.

1

2

CREAMY CHICKEN AND ZUCCHINI SOUP

Preparation time: 10 minutes
Total cooking time: 10 minutes
Serves 4

20 g (¾ oz) butter
3 skinless, boneless chicken breasts, thinly sliced
800 g (1 lb 12 oz) zucchini (courgettes), grated
1 onion, grated
2 garlic cloves, crushed
2 tablespoons plain (all-purpose) flour
750 ml (26 fl oz/3 cups) chicken stock
250 ml (9 fl oz/1 cup) cream

1 Melt the butter in a large saucepan, add the chicken and cook over medium heat for 1–2 minutes, or until the chicken changes colour. Add the zucchini, onion and garlic, and cook, stirring occasionally, for 5 minutes.
2 Stir in the flour and cook for 1 minute. Add the stock, bring to the boil, stirring until it boils and thickens slightly. Reduce the heat and simmer for 1 minute. Stir in the cream and cook for 2 minutes. Season and serve.

1

2

LENTIL AND VEGETABLE SOUP

Preparation time: 10 minutes
Total cooking time: 20 minutes
Serves 4–6

8 spring onions (scallions)
2 tablespoons oil
3 teaspoons curry powder
1.25 litres (5 cups) vegetable stock
250 g (9 oz/1 cup) red lentils
425 g (15 oz) tinned tomatoes
250 g (9 oz) broccoli, chopped
2 zucchini (courgettes), sliced

1 Trim ends from spring onions and chop. Heat oil in medium pan; add spring onions. Add curry powder; stir over medium heat for 5 minutes.
2 Add stock, lentils and undrained, crushed tomatoes; bring to the boil. Reduce heat to low, simmer, covered, for 15 minutes or until lentils are tender. Stir occasionally to prevent sticking.
3 Add the broccoli and zucchini; simmer for another 5 minutes or until vegetables are tender.

COOK'S FILE

Storage time: This recipe can be made up to 3 days before required. Store, covered, in refrigerator. Soup may thicken on cooling as the lentils absorb the stock. If necessary, add a little water or vegetable stock to soup when reheating.
Variations: Brown, green, or yellow lentils are also suitable for this recipe. Cooking times may vary.

Substitute other vegetables such as carrots or beans if you prefer. Vary cooking times accordingly.

1

2

3

LAMB AND PASTA SOUP

Preparation time: 10 minutes
Total cooking time: 40 minutes
Serves 6–8

2 onions, finely chopped
2 tablespoons oil
500 g (1 lb 2 oz) lean lamb meat, cut into 2 cm (¾ inch) cubes
2 carrots, chopped
4 celery stalks, chopped
425 g (15 oz) tinned tomatoes
2 litres (8 cups) beef stock
270 g (9½ oz/3 cups) spiral pasta
chopped parsley, for serving

1 Heat oil in a large pan and cook cubed lamb in batches until golden brown. Remove each batch as it is done and drain on paper towels. Add onion to pan and cook for 2 minutes or until softened. Return meat to pan.
2 Add carrot and celery, undrained, crushed tomato and beef stock. Stir to combine and bring to the boil. Reduce heat to low and simmer, covered, for 15 minutes.
3 Add spiral pasta to the pan. Stir briefly to prevent pasta sticking. Simmer, uncovered, for another 15 minutes or until lamb and pasta are tender. Sprinkle with chopped parsley before serving.

COOK'S FILE

Storage time: This recipe can be made up to 3 days before required. Store, covered, in refrigerator.
Hints: Pasta can be cooked separately if you wish. Drain thoroughly and add to the soup before serving. Meat should be cooked quickly in batches to prevent it becoming tough.
Variations: For a lighter flavour, use half stock and half water. Vegetable stock may be used instead of beef. Other types of pasta such as maca-roni or shell pasta can be substituted.

1

2

3

Lentil and Vegetable Soup (top) and Lamb and Pasta Soup

LEEK AND POTATO SOUP

Preparation time: 15 minutes
Total cooking time: 25–30 minutes
Serves 4

3 rashers bacon
1 tablespoon oil
2 large leeks, sliced
500 g (1 lb 2 oz) potatoes, peeled and chopped
1 litre (4 cups) chicken stock

1 Chop bacon, discard rind. Heat oil in a medium pan. Add the bacon and stir over medium heat for 3 minutes or until it is lightly golden. Drain on paper towel.
2 Add leek to pan. Stir over medium heat for 5–10 minutes until soft. Add potato and stock, bring to the boil. Reduce heat to low and cover. Simmer, stirring occasionally, for 20 minutes or until potato is tender.
3 Remove pan from heat; allow mixture to cool slightly. Transfer mixture, in batches, to food processor or blender and process until smooth.
4 Return mixture to pan and add bacon, salt and pepper. Heat through and serve. Garnish with a sprig of fresh herbs, if desired.

COOK'S FILE

Storage time: This recipe can be made up to 3 days before required. Store, covered, in refrigerator.
Hint: Discard dark green tops of the leeks as they are tough. Use only the white and pale green parts. Wash leeks thoroughly before use to remove dirt and grit.

CREAMY POTATO AND SILVERBEET SOUP

Preparation time: 10 minutes
Total cooking time: 10 minutes
Serves 4

1.25 litres (5 cups) chicken stock
750 g (1 lb 10 oz) potatoes, peeled and chopped
500 g (1 lb 2 oz) silverbeet (Swiss chard)
185 g (6½ oz/¾ cup) sour cream
4 tablespoons Parmesan cheese. grated

1 Place chicken stock and potato in a large pan and bring stock to the boil. Cover pan; reduce heat to low and simmer mixture for 5 minutes or until potato is almost tender.

2 Wash silverbeet thoroughly; drain. Using a sharp knife, remove stalks from silverbeet. Shred leaves and add to pan. Simmer, covered, for 3 minutes or until potato and silverbeet are tender Add sour cream and Parmesan cheese and stir thoroughly to combine. Remove pan from heat.

3 Transfer mixture to food processor or blender in small batches. Process each batch until smooth. Return mixture to pan, stir over medium heat for 1 minute or until heated through. Garnish with chive flowers or other fresh herbs, if desired.

COOK'S FILE

Storage time: This soup can be made up to 2 days before required. Store, covered, in refrigerator.

1

2

ASIAN CHICKEN NOODLE SOUP

Preparation time: 10 minutes
Total cooking time: 10 minutes
Serves 4

85 g (3 oz) fresh egg noodles
1.25 litres (42 fl oz/5 cups) chicken stock
1 tablespoon mirin (see Note)
2 tablespoons soy sauce
3 cm (1¼ inch) piece fresh ginger, peeled and thinly sliced
2 skinless, boneless chicken breasts, thinly sliced
2 bunches baby bok choy (pak choy), stalks trimmed
coriander (cilantro) leaves, to garnish

1

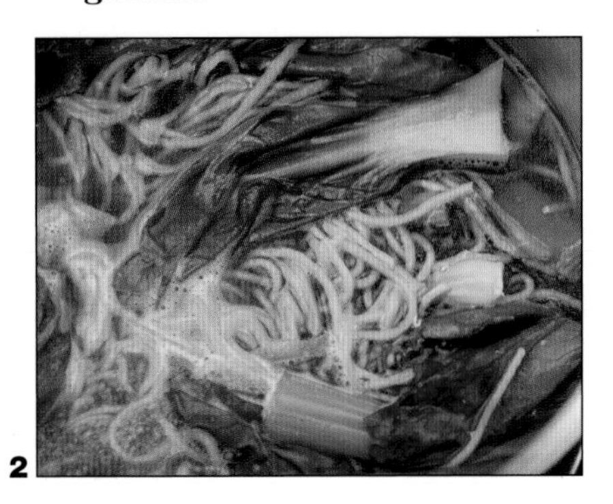
2

1 Soak the noodles in boiling water for 1 minute, drain and set aside. In a large saucepan, heat the stock to simmering, add the mirin, soy sauce, ginger, chicken and noodles. Cook for 5 minutes, or until the chicken is tender and the noodles are warmed through. Remove any scum from the surface of the soup.

2 Add the bok choy and cook for 2 minutes, or until the bok choy has wilted. Serve garnished with coriander. Serve with sweet chilli sauce, if desired.

COOK'S FILE

Note: Mirin is a sweet rice wine used for cooking. Sweet sherry, with a little sugar added, can be used instead.

LOW-FAT SEAFOOD LAKSA

Preparation time: 15 minutes + 10 minutes soaking
Total cooking time: 10 minutes
Serves 4

150 g (5½ oz) dried rice vermicelli
3 tablespoons good-quality laksa paste
250 ml (9 fl oz/1 cup) low-fat coconut milk
1 litre (34 fl oz/4 cups) fish or vegetable stock
12 large raw prawns (shrimp), peeled and deveined, with tails intact
250 g (9 oz) firm white fish fillets (ling or blue eye), cut into 3 cm (1¼ inch) cubes
200 g (7 oz) squid rings
1½ tablespoons lime juice
1½ tablespoons fish sauce
3 tablespoons chopped coriander (cilantro) leaves
100 g (3½ oz) bean sprouts
1 lime, cut into quarters
coriander (cilantro) leaves, extra, to garnish

1 Soak the noodles in hot water for 10 minutes. Drain and set aside.

2 Heat a large wok and when very hot, add the laksa paste. Stir-fry for 1 minute, then add the coconut milk. Bring to the boil, then reduce the heat. Add the stock and simmer for another minute before adding the prawns and fish. Cook for 4 minutes, or until the prawns and fish have turned opaque, then stir in the squid rings, lime juice, fish sauce and the chopped coriander. Cook for a further 1–2 minutes.

3 To serve, run the noodles under hot water to separate, then divide among four serving bowls. Top the noodles with the bean sprouts and pour on the soup–each bowl should get three prawns. Garnish with a wedge of lime and extra coriander leaves.

Peel the prawns and pull out the dark vein from the back, leaving the tail intact.

Stir-fry the laksa paste for 1 minute in a very hot wok.

Cook the prawns and fish in the coconut milk and stock until they turn opaque.

Salads and light meals

TUNA AND CANNELLINI BEAN SALAD

185 g (6½ oz) tin good-quality tuna in oil, drained (reserving 1 tablespoon oil)
400 g (14 oz) tin cannellini beans, rinsed and drained
½ small red onion, sliced
1 tablespoon baby capers, rinsed and drained
100 g (3½ oz) semi-dried (sun-blushed) tomatoes in oil (reserving 2 tablespoons oil)
75 g (2½ oz) baby rocket (arugula) leaves
3 tablespoons fresh basil, chopped
1–1½ tablespoons tarragon vinegar

Toss the tuna, cannellini beans, onion, capers, semi-dried tomatoes, rocket leaves and basil together in a bowl. Whisk the tarragon vinegar and the reserved oils together in a seperate bowl until well combined, pour over the salad, toss again and season with salt and pepper. Serves 4.

CHICKEN, AVOCADO AND BACON SALAD

2 skinless, boneless chicken breasts (about 350 g/12 oz each), trimmed of excess fat
3½ tablespoons olive oil
3 rashers bacon, cut into thin strips
2 Roma (plum) tomatoes, sliced
110 g (3¾ oz) mixed lettuce
1 avocado, cut into slices
1 tablespoon balsamic vinegar
50 g (1¾ oz/½ cup) shaved Parmesan

Season the chicken well on both sides. Heat 1 tablespoon of the oil in a frying pan and cook the chicken over medium heat for 4–5 minutes on each side, or until golden brown and cooked through. Keep warm. Cook the bacon in the same pan for 4 minutes, or until crisp and golden. Drain on paper towels. Gently toss the tomato, lettuce, avocado and bacon together in a bowl. Cut the chicken on the diagonal into thin slices, then add to the salad. Whisk the vinegar and the remaining oil together until well combined, pour over the salad and toss again. Season. Garnish with Parmesan and serve immediately. Serves 4.

ROASTED VEGETABLE AND HALOUMI SALAD

2 small red capsicums (peppers), cut into 3 cm (1¼ inch) pieces
2 zucchini (courgettes), cut on the diagonal into 1 cm (½ inch) slices
6 slender eggplants (aubergines), cut on the diagonal into 1 cm (½ inch) slices
4 Roma (plum) tomatoes, cut into quarters
8 whole garlic cloves, unpeeled
3½ tablespoons olive oil
1 tablespoon red wine vinegar
250 g (9 oz) haloumi cheese, cut into 1 cm (½ inch) slices
fresh flat-leaf (Italian) parsley, chopped, to garnish
fresh mint, finely chopped, to garnish

Preheat the oven to 190°C (375°F/Gas 5). Toss all of the vegetables in a large roasting tin with the garlic and 2 tablespoons of the olive oil. Season well. Roast for 40 minutes, or until the vegetables are tender and golden. Whisk the vinegar and the remaining olive oil together until well combined. Arrange the vegetables on a large serving platter and keep warm. Heat a chargrill pan or barbecue plate to very hot, then cook the haloumi for 1–2 minutes on each side, or until dark grill lines appear. Remove and place around the roasted vegetables. Drizzle with the dressing and garnish with the parsley and mint. Serves 4.

GREEK PEPPERED LAMB SALAD

300 g (10½ oz) lamb backstraps
1½ tablespoons black pepper
3 vine-ripened tomatoes, cut into 8 wedges
2 Lebanese (short) cucumbers, sliced
150 g (5½ oz) lemon and garlic marinated Kalamata olives, drained (reserving 1½ tablespoons oil)
100 g (3½ oz) Greek feta, cubed
¾ teaspoon dried oregano
1 tablespoon lemon juice
1 tablespoon extra virgin olive oil

Roll the backstraps in the pepper, pressing the pepper on with your fingers. Cover and refrigerate for 15 minutes. Place the tomato, cucumber, olives, feta and ½ teaspoon of the dried oregano in a bowl. Heat a chargrill pan (griddle) or barbecue plate, brush with oil and when very hot, cook the lamb for 2–3 minutes on each side, or until cooked to your liking. Keep warm. Whisk the lemon juice, extra virgin olive oil, reserved Kalamata oil and the remaining dried oregano together. Season. Pour half the dressing over the salad, toss together and arrange on a serving platter. Cut the lamb on the diagonal into 1 cm (½ inch) thick slices and arrange on top of the salad. Pour the remaining dressing on top and serve. Serves 4.

CAESAR SALAD

Preparation time: 15 minutes
Total cooking time: 15 minutes
Serves 4

4 slices white bread
3 bacon rashers, chopped
1 cos (romaine) lettuce
50 g (1¾ oz/½ cup) shaved Parmesan cheese

Dressing
4 anchovies, chopped
1 legg
1–2 tablespoons lemon juice
1 garlic clove, crushed
125 ml (4 fl oz/½ cup) oil

1 Preheat oven to 210°C (415°F/Gas 6–7). Remove crusts from bread, cut bread into small cubes. Spread on a baking tray and bake for 15 minutes or until lightly golden. Fry bacon until crisp. Drain on paper towel. Tear lettuce leaves into bite-sized pieces. Combine in a bowl with bread cubes, Parmesan and bacon. Add the dressing, toss until combined, serve immediately.

2 To make the dressing, place anchovies, egg, lemon juice and garlic in food processor or blender. Blend for 20 seconds or until smooth. With motor constantly operating, add oil slowly in a thin, steady stream, processing until all oil is added and dressing is thick and creamy.

COOK'S FILE

Storage time: Bread cubes can be baked a day in advance. Store in an airtight container. Dressing can also be made a day in advance and refrigerated in an airtight container. Assemble salad just before serving.

Hint: Use a vegetable peeler to make Parmesan cheese shavings.

CHEF'S SALAD

Preparation time: 15 minutes
Total cooking time: Nil
Serves 4

200 g (7 oz) mixed lettuce leaves (see Note)
250 g (9 oz) leg ham, cut into strips
125 g (4¼ oz) Swiss cheese slices, cut into strips
1 red capsicum (pepper), cut into strips
340 g (12 oz) tin asparagus cuts, drained (see Variation)

Dressing
3 tablespoon mayonnaise
3 tablespoons cream
1 tablespoon seeded mustard

1 Arrange lettuce, ham, cheese, capsicum and asparagus on four serving plates.
2 To make dressing; whisk the mayonnaise, cream and mustard for 1 minute or until combined. Drizzle dressing over salad before serving.

1

COOK'S FILE

Note: Mixed lettuce is available from greengrocers. However, any variety of lettuce is suitable for this salad.
Variation: Use blanched, fresh asparagus instead, of tinned asparagus, if preferred.

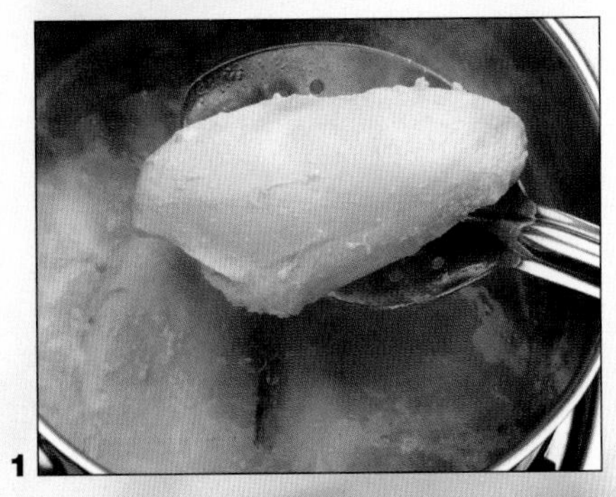

1

2

3

VIETNAMESE-STYLE CHICKEN AND CABBAGE SALAD

Preparation time: 15 minutes
Total cooking time: 10 minutes
Serves 4

3 skinless, boneless chicken breasts
1 red chilli, deseeded, membrane removed, finely chopped
3 tablespoons lime juice
2 tablespoons soft brown sugar
3 tablespoons fish sauce
½ Chinese cabbage, shredded
2 carrots, grated
50 g (1¾ oz/1 cup) shredded mint

1 Put the chicken in a saucepan, cover with water and bring to the boil, then reduce the heat and simmer for 10 minutes, or until cooked through.
2 While the chicken is cooking, mix together the chilli, lime juice, sugar and fish sauce. Remove the chicken from the water. Cool slightly, then shred into small pieces.
3 Combine the chicken, cabbage, carrot, mint and dressing. Toss well and serve immediately.

COOK'S FILE

Hint: Any leftovers can be used the next day in a stir-fry.

CHICKEN, BLUE CHEESE AND WALNUT SALAD

Preparation time: 15 minutes
Total cooking time: 20 minutes
Serves 4

2 large skineless, boneless chicken breasts
4 tablespoons olive oil
3 teaspoons dried French tarragon
60 g (2¼ oz/½ cup) walnuts, chopped
2 tablespoons cider vinegar
1 teaspoon Dijon mustard
100 g (3½ oz) baby English spinach leaves
125 g (4½ oz) firm blue cheese, crumbled

1 Preheat the oven to 170°C (325°F/ Gas 3). Place the chicken breasts on a foil-lined baking tray. Brush with half the oil and sprinkle generously with freshly ground black pepper and 1 teaspoon dried tarragon. Cook under a hot griller (broiler) for 10 minutes, turning once. Meanwhile, place the walnuts on an oven tray and roast for 10 minutes, or until lightly golden.
2 To make the dressing, whisk together the remaining tarragon, vinegar and Dijon mustard with the remaining olive oil. Season to taste.
3 Cut the chicken across the grain into 1.5 cm (⅝ inch) thick strips. Put the spinach, chicken, walnuts and blue cheese in a large serving bowl, add the dressing, toss and serve immediately.

COOK'S FILE

Note: The chicken can be increased to 4 breasts to serve as a light dinner.

1

2

3

SALAD NIÇOISE

Preparation time: 10 minutes
Total cooking time: 10 minutes
Serves 4

16 baby potatoes
250 g (9 oz) green beans, sliced into short pieces
250 g (9 oz) cherry tomatoes, quartered
115 g (4 oz/⅔ cup) black olives
425 g (15 oz) can tuna, drained and flaked
100 g (3½ oz) feta cheese, cubed
8 anchovies, chopped
4 tablespoons Italian dressing
4 hard-boiled eggs, quartered
1 lettuce, for serving

1 Cook potatoes in large pan of rapidly boiling water for 10 minutes or until tender; drain, cool.
2 Cook beans in medium pan of rapidly boiling water for 3 minutes or until tender; drain, cool. Cut potatoes into quarters.
3 Place potato quarters and beans in large bowl with tomato, olives, tuna, cheese, anchovies and dressing; stir until combined. Add eggs; stir gently to mix. Serve on a bed of lettuce.

COOK'S FILE

Storage time: Salad can be assembled several hours ahead. Store, covered, in refrigerator. Add dressing just before serving.
Note: Use home-made or commercial Italian dressing for this recipe.

1

WARM BEAN SALAD

Preparation time: 10 minutes
Total cooking time: 8 minutes
Serves 4

2 tablespoons olive oil
1 medium onion, finely chopped
1 clove garlic, crushed
1 small red capsicum (pepper), cut into short strips
75 g (2½ oz) green beans, cut into 2 cm (¾ inch) lengths
50 g (1¾ oz) button mushrooms, sliced
1 tablespoon balsamic vinegar
430 g (15 oz) tin three-bean mix

1 Heat half the oil in a pan. Add onion and cook for 2 minutes over medium heat. Add garlic, capsicum, green beans, mushrooms and vinegar. Cook for another 5 minutes, stirring occasionally.

2 Thoroughly rinse and drain bean mix. Add to vegetables with remaining oil, stir until just warmed through.

COOK'S FILE

Storage time: May be kept for 1 day in refrigerator. Reheat for serving.

Hint: This salad is delicious as an accompaniment to roast lamb. Serve with toasted thick Italian bread for a vegetarian main meal.

WARM THAI BEEF SALAD

Preparation time: 15 minutes
Total cooking time: 10 minutes
Serves 4

400 g (14 oz) beef fillet steaks
75 g (2½ oz) mixed salad leaves
½ small red onion, thinly sliced
100 g (3½ oz) cherry tomatoes, halved
1 small Lebanese (short) cucumber, thinly sliced
4 tablespoons chopped coriander (cilantro) leaves
4 tablespoons chopped mint

Dressing
1½ tablespoons fish sauce
2 tablespoons lime juice
1 tablespoon soft brown sugar
1 small red chilli, deseeded and finely chopped

1 Season the beef well on both sides with freshly ground black pepper. Spray a chargrill pan (griddle) or barbecue hotplate with oil spray and when very hot, sear the beef fillets on each side for 3–4 minutes. Season with salt. Remove and leave to rest for 10 minutes. Slice beef thinly—meat should still be quite pink in middle.

2 While the meat is resting, make the dressing. Combine the fish sauce, lime juice, brown sugar, chilli and 2 tablespoons water in a small saucepan and stir over low heat until the sugar has dissolved. Remove from the heat and keep warm.

3 Place the mixed salad leaves, onion, tomatoes, cucumber, coriander leaves and mint in a large bowl and toss together. Arrange the salad on a large platter, top with the beef slices and pour the warm dressing on top. Serve immediately.

Press freshly ground black pepper onto the fillets with your fingertips.

Allow the steaks to rest, then slice thinly using a sharp knife.

Toss together the mixed salad leaves, onion, tomato, cucumber, coriander and mint.

CHICKEN SALAD WITH HONEY-GLAZED SWEET POTATO

Preparation time: 15 minutes
Total cooking time: 30 minutes
Serves 4

1.2 kg (2 lb 11 oz) orange sweet potato, peeled and sliced
1 tablespoon honey
1 tablespoon oil
4 skinless, boneless chicken breasts
2–3 tablespoons lemon juice
2 tablespoons olive oil
160 g (5½ oz) baby English spinach leaves
200 g (7 oz) feta cheese, diced

1 Preheat the oven to 200°C (400°F/Gas 6). Place the sweet potato on a baking tray. Drizzle with the combined honey and oil to coat well and roast for 20 minutes, or until soft.

2 Heat a non-stick frying pan over medium heat, add the chicken breasts and cook for 3–4 minutes each side, or until cooked through. Alternatively, sear the breasts and then place in the oven with the sweet potato for 10 minutes, or until cooked through. Leave to cool slightly and then slice into thin strips across the grain.

3 Mix together the lemon juice and olive oil to make the dressing. Place the spinach leaves in a bowl, add the sweet potato, feta and chicken, and season. Pour the dressing over the salad, toss to coat the leaves and serve.

COOK'S FILE

Note: The sweet potato and the chicken can be cooked ahead of time and all the ingredients tossed together when you are ready to eat.

1

2

3

Jacket Potatoes

There's nothing quite as satisfying as a baked potato with toppings. Full of carbohydrates and fibre, the potato itself has many good nutritional qualities. Remember, it's the lashings of full-fat cheese and sour cream that will send the fat meter soaring, so try these low-fat ideas instead.

BAKING YOUR POTATO

Preheat the oven to 210°C (415°F/ Gas 6–7). Scrub 4 large potatoes clean, dry and pierce all over with a fork. Bake directly on the oven rack for 1 hour, or until tender when tested with a skewer. Leave to stand for about 2 minutes. Cut a cross in the top of each cooked potato and squeeze gently from the base to open (if the potato is still too hot, hold the potato in a clean tea towel). The following toppings all serve 4.

AVOCADO TOMATO AND CORN SALSA

Remove the seeds from 2 vine-ripened tomatoes and chop. Place the tomato in a bowl with 125 g (4½ oz) tin corn kernels, 2 chopped spring onions (scallions), 1 tablespoon lime juice and ½ teaspoon sugar and mix well. Add 1 diced avocado and 3 tablespoons chopped coriander (cilantro) leaves. Season. Spoon mixture onto each potato and, if desired, dollop with 1 tablespoon low-fat sour cream.

MUSHROOM AND BACON

Fry 3 trimmed and finely sliced bacon rashers in a non-stick frying pan until lightly golden. Add 1 clove crushed garlic, 2 chopped spring onions (scallions), 1 teaspoon chopped thyme and 180 g (6 oz/2 cups) sliced button mushrooms. Cook over high heat for 3–4 minutes, or until the liquid has evaporated. Add 185 g (6½ oz/ ¾ cup) low-fat sour cream and season well. Reduce the heat to low. Cook for one further minute. Stir in 2 tablespoons chopped parsley. Spoon the mixture onto each potato. Sprinkle with extra chopped parsley and grated low-fat cheese.

COTTAGE PIE POTATOES

Spray a deep frying pan lightly with oil spray. Place over medium heat. Add 1 finely chopped onion, 1 clove crushed garlic, 1 chopped carrot and 1 chopped celery stick. Cook until just soft. Add 250 g (9 oz) lean minced (ground) lamb. Cook for 2–3 minutes, or until it changes colour. Add 400 g

(14 oz) canned tomatoes, 1 tablespoon Worcestershire sauce, 1 tablespoon tomato paste (concentrated purée) and 125 ml (4 fl oz/½ cup) water. Cook for 20–25 minutes, or until thickened and reduced. Add 80 g (2¾/½ cup) frozen peas and 2 tablespoons chopped parsley. Simmer for another 5 minutes. Season. Spoon the mixture onto each potato and serve.

CHICKEN, ROCKET AND BABY CAPER SALAD

Bring 500 ml (17 fl oz/2 cups) chicken stock to the boil in a small saucepan. Add 2 chicken breasts, reduce the heat and simmer, covered, for 5 minutes. Remove the pan from the heat and cool the chicken breasts in the liquid. Shred the meat into a bowl. Add 2 tablespoons low-fat mayonnaise, 1 teaspoon grated lemon zest and 1 tablespoon baby capers. Season. Toss 135 g (4¾ oz/3 cups) roughly shredded rocket (arugula) with 1 tablespoon extra virgin olive oil, 1 tablespoon balsamic vinegar and 1 thinly sliced avocado. Stuff into each potato. Top with the chicken mixture. Season.

SMOKED TUNA AND WHITE BEAN SALSA

Drain 100 g (3½ oz) tin smoked tuna, reserving 1 tablespoon of its oil. Heat the oil in a frying pan and cook 3 finely chopped spring onions (scallions) and 2 crushed garlic cloves over low heat for 1 minute, or until softened. Add 400 g (14 oz) tin cannellini beans (rinsed and drained) and cook for a further 3–4 minutes, or until the beans are warmed through. Remove from the heat and add 2 tablespoons chopped basil, 2 tablespoons chopped mint, 1 tablespoon lemon juice and 1 deseeded and chopped vine-ripened tomato and combine well. Add the tuna and season with salt and freshly ground black pepper. Spoon the mixture onto each potato. Garnish with low-fat sour cream and chopped fresh flat-leaf (Italian) parsley.

TABBOULEH AND HUMMUS POTATOES

Soak 3 tablespoons burghul (bulgar) in 3 tablespoons water for 15 minutes, or until all the water has been absorbed. Place in a bowl with 30 g (1 oz/½ cup) chopped parsley, 25 g (1 oz/½ cup) chopped mint, 2 finely sliced spring onions (scallions), 1 finely chopped tomato, 2 tablespoons olive oil and 2 tablespoons lemon juice. Season well with salt and freshly ground black pepper. Dollop 1–2 tablespoons low-fat hummus onto each potato and top with the tabbouleh.

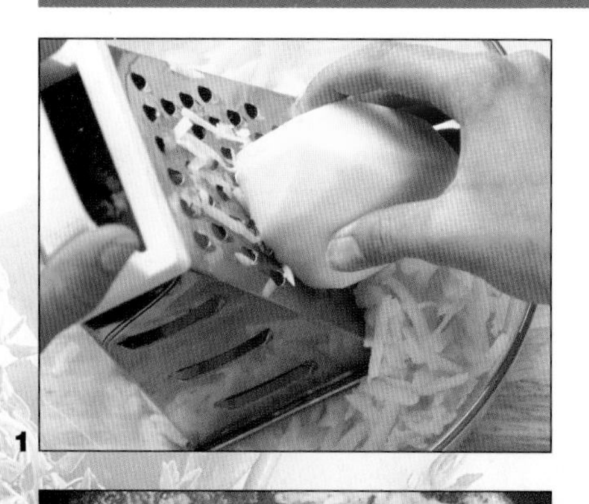

1

HERBED POTATO PANCAKES

Preparation time: 10 minutes
Total cooking time: 12 minutes
Makes 10–12 pancakes

2 tablespoons chopped chives
2 tablespoons chopped tarragon or parsley
600 g (1 lb 5 oz) potatoes, peeled
60 g (2¼ oz) unsalted butter
2 tablespoons olive oil

1 Mix chives, tarragon or parsley and salt and pepper in a bowl. Coarsely grate the potatoes into a large bowl. Add herb mixture and stir to combine.
2 Heat half the butter and oil in large non-stick frying pan, over medium heat, until starting to foam. Cook heaped tablespoons full of mixture for 2 minutes. Turn and cook for approximately 2–3 minutes or until golden. Drain on paper towels; keep warm. Add remaining butter and oil to pan. Repeat process until all mixture is used.

COOK'S FILE

Storage time: Pancakes may be kept for up to ½ hour, loosely covered with foil, in a 120°C (250°F/Gas ½) oven.
Note: Work quickly when grating potato. Potato can be grated using a food processor if preferred. Cook mixture immediately after it has been prepared to prevent the potato from discolouring. A starchy liquid will form in the bowl. Don't discard, mix into the pancakes.
Variations: Substitute parsnip or carrot for one of the potatoes.

Substitute chopped dill for the tarragon or parsley.

EGGPLANT SANDWICHES

Preparation time: 10 minutes + 30 minutes standing
Total cooking time: 20 minutes
Serves 4

3 medium eggplant (aubergines)
olive oil, for frying
ground cumin, optional
2 red capsicums (peppers), roughly chopped, deseeded and membrane removed
10–12 semi-dried (sun-blushed) tomatoes
200 g (7 oz) ricotta or goats cheese
4 tablespoons shredded basil leaves
basil leaves, extra

1 Slice eggplant lengthways, about 1 cm (½ inch) thick. Choose the 8 largest slices and lay on a tray or board. Reserve rest (see Note). Sprinkle eggplant with salt. Allow to stand for 30 minutes. Rinse well and pat dry with paper towel.

2 Heat a large frying pan over medium heat. Add oil to cover base of pan. When hot add eggplant slices, a few at a time. Cook for 2–3 minutes on each side or until brown. Drain on paper towels. Season each slice with salt and pepper. Sprinkle with cumin.

3 Place capsicums cut-side down on cold grill (broiler) tray. Brush skin with oil. Cook under preheated grill (broiler) until skin blackens and blisters. Cover with damp tea-towel (dish towel) until cool. Peel off skin and cut into strips.

4 Cut semi-dried tomatoes into strips. On each serving plate, place a slice of eggplant. Spread with ricotta or goats cheese. Top with sundried tomato and capsicum, reserving some for garnish. Sprinkle with basil. Cover each with a second slice of eggplant. Decorate top with crossed strips of capsicum and sundried tomato. Garnish with extra basil leaves.

COOK'S FILE

Note: Unused eggplant will last a day or two in refrigerator. Finely chop and brown in olive oil with crushed garlic, season well. Spread on toast for a snack or add to a soup or casserole.

1 2 3 4

SMOKED CHICKEN AND CORN FRITTERS

Preparation time: 15 minutes
Total cooking time: 15 minutes
Serves 4

90 g (3¼ oz/¾ cup) self-raising flour
1 egg, lightly beaten
170 ml (5½ fl oz/⅔ cup) milk
310 g (11 oz) tin creamed corn
100 g (3½ oz/¾ cup) smoked chicken, finely chopped
2 spring onions (scallions), sliced
1 tablespoon chopped chives
4 tablespoons extra virgin olive oil

1 Sift the flour into a large bowl. Make a well in the flour and add the egg and milk. Using a wooden spoon, gradually stir the mixture to form a smooth batter.

2 Stir in the creamed corn, chicken, spring onion and chives. Season to taste with salt and freshly ground black pepper.

3 Heat half the oil in a shallow non-stick frying pan and add heaped tablespoons of the batter, flattening the mixture out a little. Cook, in batches, over high heat for about 2 minutes each side, or until golden brown. Add the remaining oil during cooking when necessary. Drain fritters on paper towels and serve immediately with pesto or olive tapenade, or a quick sauce made from plain yoghurt and mango or other fruit chutney.

1

2

3

OMELETTE WITH ASPARAGUS, SMOKED SALMON AND DILL

Preparation time: 10 minutes
Total cooking time: 10 minutes
Serves 2

6 egg whites
6 eggs
2 tablespoons low-fat ricotta cheese
2 tablespoons chopped dill
420 g (15 oz) fresh asparagus, cut into 5 cm (2 inch) lengths
100 g (3½ oz) smoked salmon, thinly sliced
lemon wedges, to garnish
sprigs of dill, to garnish

1 Whisk the egg whites until foaming. In a separate bowl, whisk the whole eggs and ricotta until combined. Add whites. Season and stir in the dill.
2 Bring a saucepan of lightly salted water to the boil. Add the asparagus and cook for 1–2 minutes, or until tender but still firm to the bite. Drain and refresh in iced water.
3 Heat a non-stick 24 cm (9½ inch) frying pan over low heat. Spray lightly with oil spray. Pour in half the egg mixture. Arrange half the asparagus on top. Cook over medium heat until the egg is just setting. Flip one side onto the other. Transfer to a serving plate. Repeat with remaining mixture.
4 To serve, top with smoked salmon and add lemon and a sprig of dill.

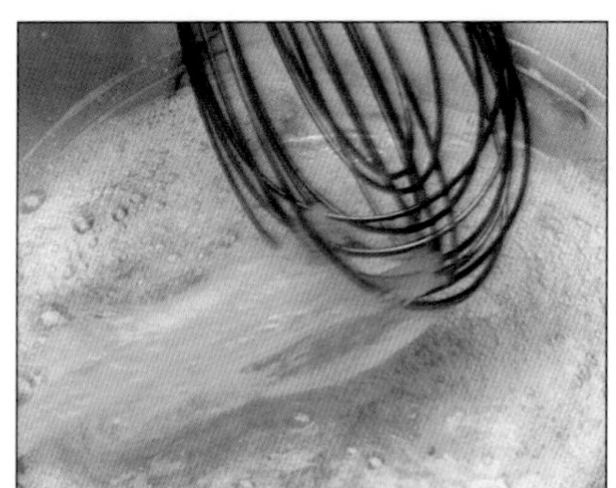

Whisk the egg whites in a clean dry bowl until foaming.

Place the asparagus pieces in iced water to stop them cooking.

Arrange half the asparagus pieces evenly over the egg mixture.

CORN AND CAPSICUM FRITTERS

Preparation time: 20 minutes
Total cooking time: 10 minutes
Serves 4

1 large red capsicum (pepper)
300 g (10½ oz) fresh corn kernels (2–3 cobs) oil, for frying
2 tablespoons chopped parsley, coriander (cilantro) leaves, chives or dill
3 eggs

1 Cut capsicum into large pieces and chop into small cubes.
2 Heat 2 tablespoons of the oil in a large frying pan. Add the corn kernels and stir over medium heat for 2 minutes. Add the red capsicum, stir for another 2 minutes. Transfer vegetables to a bowl. Add herbs and stir well to combine. Beat eggs in a small jug with pepper and salt, to taste. Stir egg gradually into the vegetable mixture.
3 Heat a non-stick frying pan over medium heat. Add oil to cover base. Drop large spoonfuls of the vegetable mixture at a time into oil. Cook 1–2 minutes or until brown. Turn; cook other side. Drain on paper towels; keep warm. Serve garnished with a parsley sprig, if desired.

COOK'S FILE

Hint: The fritters may be served with sour cream and a crisp green salad for lunch or as accompaniment to a main course.
Note: These fritters contain no flour, so they cook quickly. They should still be a little creamy in the middle when served.

1

2

3

SPICY CHICKEN PATTIES

Preparation time: 10 minutes + chilling
Total cooking time: 15 minutes
Serves 4

500 g (1 lb 2 oz) minced (ground) chicken
4 spring onions (scallions), finely chopped
4 tablespoons finely chopped coriander (cilantro) leaves
2 cloves garlic, crushed
¾ teaspoon cayenne pepper
1 egg white, lightly beaten
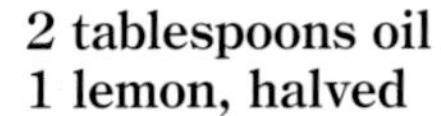
2 tablespoons oil
1 lemon, halved

1 Mix together all the ingredients except the oil and lemon, season with salt and freshly ground black pepper and shape the mixture into four patties. Refrigerate the patties for 20 minutes before cooking.
2 Heat the oil in a large frying pan over medium heat, add the patties and cook for about 5 minutes on each side, or until browned and cooked through.
3 Squeeze the lemon on the cooked patties and serve with a salad or use to make burgers.

1

2

3

Pasta

1

2

SPAGHETTINI WITH ASPARAGUS AND ROCKET

Preparation time: 15 minutes
Cooking time: 15 minutes
Serves 4

100 ml (3½ fl oz) extra virgin olive oil
16 thin asparagus spears, cut into 5 cm (2 inch) lengths
375 g (13 oz) spaghettini
120 g (4¼ oz) rocket (arugula), shredded
2 small fresh red chillies, finely chopped
2 teaspoons finely grated lemon rind
1 clove garlic, finely chopped
100 g (3½ oz/1 cup) grated Parmesan
2 tablespoons lemon juice

1 Bring a large saucepan of water to the boil over medium heat. Add 1 tablespoon of the oil and a pinch of salt to the water and blanch the asparagus for 3–4 minutes. Remove the asparagus with a slotted spoon, refresh under cold water, drain and place in a bowl. Return the water to a rapid boil and add the spaghettini. Cook the pasta according to the packet instructions until al dente. Drain and return to the pan.

2 Meanwhile, add the rocket, chilli, lemon rind, garlic and two-thirds of the Parmesan to the asparagus and mix well. Add the mixture to the cooked pasta, pour on the lemon juice and the remaining olive oil and season with salt and freshly ground black pepper. Stir well to evenly coat the pasta with the mixture. Divide among four pasta bowls, top with the remaining Parmesan and serve.

COOK'S FILE

Variation: This dish is also suitable for other types of pasta such as tagliatelle, macaroni or spiral-shaped pasta.

PENNE WITH TOMATO AND ONION JAM WITH OLIVES

Preparation time: 15 minutes
Cooking time: 1 hour
Serves 4

3 tablespoons olive oil
4 red onions (650 g/1 lb 7oz), sliced
1 tablespoon soft brown sugar
2 tablespoons balsamic vinegar
2 x 400 g (14 oz) tins tomatoes
500 g (1 lb 2 oz) penne rigate
150 g (5½ oz) small pitted black olives or pitted and halved Kalamata olives
75 g (2½ oz/¾ cup) shaved Parmesan

1 Heat the oil in a non-stick frying pan over medium heat. Add the onion and sugar and cook for 25–30 minutes, or until caramelized.

2 Stir in the vinegar, bring to the boil and cook for 5 minutes. Add the tomatoes, return to the boil, then reduce the heat to medium–low and simmer for 25 minutes, or until the tomatoes are reduced and jam-like.

3 Meanwhile, cook the pasta in a large saucepan of rapidly boiling salted water (according to the packet) instructions until al dente. Drain, then return to the pan. Add the tomato mixture and olives and stir to combine. Season to taste with salt and black pepper and serve with Parmesan shavings.

COOK'S FILE

Notes: Caramelized onions will keep for a few days if covered with oil and stored in the refrigerator.

The onions can be combined with goat's cheese to make a quick puff pastry tart, used as a pizza topping, or to accompany a steak sandwich.

1

2

1

2

TORTELLINI WITH EGGPLANT SAUCE

Preparation time: 10 minutes
Total cooking time: 20 minutes
Serves 4

500 g (1 lb 2 oz) fresh tortellini
3 tablespoons oil
2 garlic cloves, crushed
1 red capsicum (pepper), chopped
500 g (1 lb 2 oz) eggplant (aubergine), chopped
425 g (15 oz) tin tomatoes
250 ml (9 fl oz/1 cup) vegetable stock
30 g (1 oz/½ cup) chopped basil

1 Add tortellini to a large pan of rapidly boiling water and cook until just tender. Drain pasta. Heat oil in a large pan; add garlic and capsicum. Stir over medium heat for 1 minute.

2 Add eggplant cubes and stir over medium heat for 5 minutes or until lightly browned. Add to pan the undrained, crushed tomatoes and vegetable stock. Stir to combine and bring to the boil. Reduce heat to low and cover pan; cook for 10 minutes or until vegetables are tender. Add basil and drained pasta and stir until well combined. Serve.

COOK'S FILE

Storage time: Sauce can be made a day ahead. Store, covered, in refrigerator. Cook pasta and reheat sauce just before serving.

Hints: Cut the eggplant just before using as it turns brown when exposed to the air.

SALMON AND PASTA MORNAY

Preparation time: 10 minutes
Total cooking time: 10–15 minutes
Serves 4

400 g (14 oz) small shell pasta
30 g (1 oz) butter
6 spring onions (scallions), chopped
2 garlic cloves, crushed
1 tablespoon plain (all-purpose) flour
250 ml (9 fl oz/1 cup) milk
250 g (9 oz/1 cup) sour cream
1 tablespoon lemon juice
425 g (15 oz) tin salmon, drained, flaked
30 g (1 oz/½ cup) chopped parsley

1 Add pasta to a large pan of rapidly boiling water and cook until just tender; drain.

2 While pasta is cooking, melt butter in medium pan; add onion and garlic. Stir over low heat for 3 minutes or until tender. Add flour and stir for 1 minute. Combine milk, cream and lemon juice in a jug. Add gradually to onion mixture, stirring constantly. Stir over medium heat for 3 minutes or until mixture boils and thickens.

3 Add salmon and parsley to pan; stir for 1 minute or until heated through. Turn hotplate off. Add drained pasta to pan, stir until well combined. Season with salt and pepper before serving.

COOK'S FILE

Storage time: Sauce can be made a day ahead. Store, covered, in refrigerator. Cook pasta and reheat sauce just before serving.

1 2

PASTA WITH PORK AND FENNEL SAUSAGES

Preparation time: 15 minutes
Cooking time: 40 minutes
Serves 4

6 Italian pork and fennel sausages (about 550 g/ 1 lb 4 oz)
1 tablespoon olive oil
1 small red onion, finely chopped
2–3 garlic cloves, crushed
½ teaspoon chilli flakes
300 g (10½ oz) field or button mushrooms, thinly sliced
2 x 400 g (14 oz) tins diced tomatoes
1 tablespoon finely chopped fresh thyme
500 g (1 lb 2 oz) penne rigate
grated Parmesan, to serve

1 Split the sausages open, remove and crumble the filling, then discard the skins.

2 Heat the oil in a large saucepan over medium–high heat and cook the onion for 3–4 minutes, or until fragrant and transparent. Add the garlic, chilli flakes, mushrooms and crumbled sausage meat. Cook over high heat, stirring gently to mash the sausage meat, for 4–5 minutes, or until the meat is evenly browned. If necessary, use a tablespoon to remove any excess fat from the pan, leaving about a tablespoon of oil. Continue to cook, stirring once or twice, for 10 minutes. Stir in the tomato and thyme, then bring the sauce to the boil. Cover and cook over medium–low heat for 20 minutes, stirring occasionally to make sure the sauce doesn't stick to the bottom of the pan.

3 Meanwhile, cook the pasta in a large saucepan of rapidly boiling salted water according to the packet instructions until al dente. Drain well, then add to the sauce, stirring gently to combine. Garnish with Parmesan, then serve immediately with a green salad.

1

2

LEMON THYME TUNA WITH TAGLIATELLE

Preparation time: 15 minutes
Cooking time: 15 minutes
Serves 4

375 g (13 oz) tagliatelle
140 ml (4½ fl oz) extra virgin olive oil
1 small fresh red chilli, deseeded and finely chopped
3 tablespoons drained capers
1½ tablespoons fresh lemon thyme leaf tips
500 g (1 lb 2 oz) tuna steaks, trimmed and cut into 3 cm (1¼ inch) cubes
3 tablespoons lemon juice
1 tablespoon grated lemon rind
30 g (1 oz/½ cup) chopped fresh flat-leaf (Italian) parsley

1 Cook the pasta in a large saucepan of rapidly boiling salted water according to the packet instructions until al dente. Drain, then return to the pan.

2 Meanwhile, heat 1 tablespoon of the oil in a large frying pan. Add the chilli and capers and cook, stirring, for 1 minute, or until the capers are crisp. Add the thyme and cook for another minute. Transfer to a bowl.

3 Heat another tablespoon of oil in the pan. Add the tuna cubes and toss for 2–3 minutes, or until evenly browned on the outside but still pink in the centre—check with the point of a sharp knife. Remove from the heat.

4 Add the tuna to the caper mixture along with the lemon juice, lemon rind, parsley and the remaining oil, stirring gently until combined. Toss through the pasta, season with freshly ground black pepper and serve immediately.

1

2

TAGLIATELLE WITH MUSHROOMS

Preparation time: 10 minutes
Total cooking time: 10–15 minutes
Serves 4

375 g (13 oz) tagliatelle
1 tablespoon oil
400 g (14 oz) button mushrooms
4 rashers bacon, chopped
1 onion, chopped
310 ml (10¾ fl oz/1¼ cups) thick (double/heavy) cream
freshly grated Parmesan cheese

1 Add pasta to a large pan of rapidly boiling water and cook until just tender; drain.

2 While pasta is cooking, slice mushrooms. Heat oil in pan; add bacon and onion. Stir over medium heat for 4 minutes or until brown. Add mushrooms and stir for another 2 minutes or until tender. Add cream and stir for 1 minute or until simmering. Remove pan from heat. Add tagliatelle to sauce, stir until combined. Serve with, freshly grated Parmesan cheese.

1

COOK'S FILE

Storage time: Sauce can be made several hours ahead. Store, covered, in the refrigerator. Reheat just before serving.

Variation: Chopped pancetta can be used instead of bacon, if preferred.

POTATO GNOCCHI WITH TOMATO-OLIVE SAUCE

Preparation time: 10 minutes
Total cooking time: 15 minutes
Serves 4

500 g (1 lb 2 oz) potato gnocchi
2 tablespoons oil
1 leek, sliced
250 g (9 oz/1 cup) tomato pasta sauce
170 ml (5½ fl oz/⅔ cup) vegetable stock
4 tablespoons chopped black olives
6 anchovies, chopped

1 Add gnocchi to a large pan of rapidly boiling water and cook until just tender; drain.
2 While gnocchi is cooking, heat oil in a large pan, add leek. Stir over medium heat for 2 minutes or until tender. Add tomato sauce, stock, olives and anchovies. Stir mixture over medium heat for 5 minutes or until heated through. Serve sauce poured over gnocchi.

1

COOK'S FILE

Storage time: Sauce can be cooked a day ahead. Store, covered, in refrigerator. Reheat just before serving.
Note: Potato gnocchi is available fresh from supermarkets and delicatessens. Use any other dried or fresh pasta, if preferred.

LINGUINE WITH CHARGRILLED BASIL AND LEMON SEAFOOD

Preparation time: 15 minutes + 10 minutes marinating
Cooking time: 15 minutes
Serves 4

16 raw medium prawns (shrimp), peeled and deveined, with tails intact
350 g (12 oz) calamari rings
125 ml (4 fl oz/½ cup) extra virgin olive oil
4 tablespoons lemon juice
3 garlic cloves, crushed
½ teaspoon chilli flakes
3 tablespoons chopped fresh basil
400 g (14 oz) linguine
1 teaspoon grated lemon rind

1 Place the prawns and calamari in a non-metallic dish. To make the dressing, combine the olive oil and lemon juice in a small jug, then pour 3 tablespoons into a small bowl, reserving the rest. Stir the garlic, chilli flakes and 2 tablespoons of the basil into the bowl, pour over the seafood and mix to coat well. Cover with plastic wrap and marinate in the refrigerator for 5–10 minutes.
2 Cook the pasta in a large saucepan of rapidly boiling salted water according to the packet instructions until al dente. Drain, then return to the pan.
3 Meanwhile, preheat a chargrill (griddle) pan to high and brush with oil. Remove the prawns from the marinade with tongs and cook for 2–3 minutes each side, or until pink and cooked through. Remove. Add the calamari in batches and cook, turning once, for 1–3 minutes, or until opaque and cooked through—take care not to overcrowd the chargrill pan.
4 Transfer the pasta to a large serving bowl, then add the seafood, lemon rind and reserved dressing, and gently toss together until the linguine is well coated. Garnish with the remaining basil and season to taste. Serve with a rocket (arugula) salad.

COOK'S FILE

Note: Save time by using pre-peeled raw prawns from the seafood supplier.
Variation: Toss 1 peeled, deseeded and diced tomato through the pasta with the dressing.

ROASTED VEGETABLE CANNELLONI

Preparation time: 15 minutes
Cooking time: 40 minutes
Serves 4

60 g (2¼ oz) butter
1 large leek, cut into 1 cm (½ inch) pieces
200 g (7 oz) purchased chargrilled eggplant (aubergine)
200 g (7 oz) purchased chargrilled orange sweet potato
125 g (4½ oz/1 cup) firmly packed grated cheddar cheese
4 tablespoons plain (all-purpose) flour
1 litre (4 cups) milk
6 fresh lasagne sheets

1 Preheat the oven to 200°C (400°F/ Gas 6) and lightly grease a large ceramic dish 28 cm x 18 cm x 5 cm (11¼ inches x 7 inches x 2 inches). Melt 20 g (¾ oz) of the butter in a saucepan, add the leek and cook, stirring, over medium heat for 8 minutes, or until softened. Meanwhile, chop the eggplant and sweet potato into 1 cm (½ inch) pieces and place in a bowl. Mix in the leek and one-third of the cheddar.

2 Melt the remaining butter in a saucepan over medium heat. Stir in the flour and cook for 1 minute, or until foaming. Remove from the heat and gradually stir in the milk. Return to the heat and stir until the sauce boils and thickens. Reduce the heat and simmer for 2 minutes. Season with salt and freshly ground black pepper. Stir 375 ml (13 fl oz/1½ cups) of the sauce into the vegetable mixture, adding a little extra if necessary to bind it all together.

3 Cut the rectangular lasagne sheets in half, down the centre. Spoon some of the vegetable mixture along the centre of one sheet and roll up. Repeat with the remaining pasta sheets and vegetable mixture to make 12 tubes in total.

4 Place the tubes, seam-side-down, in the prepared dish and spoon the remaining white sauce over the top until they are completely covered. Sprinkle with the remaining cheese and bake for about 20 minutes, or until the cheese is golden brown.

COOK'S FILE

Note: Try to buy chargrilled vegetables in oil rather than dressing so it will not change the flavour of the dish.

1

2

3

SPIRAL PASTA WITH BROCCOLI AND HAM

Preparation time: 10 minutes
Total cooking time: 10–15 minutes
Serves 4

400 g (14 oz) spiral pasta
250 g (9 oz) broccoli florets
30 g (1 oz) butter
250 g (9 oz) leg ham, cut into strips
2 garlic cloves, crushed
6 spring onions (scallions), chopped
200 g (7 oz) mushrooms, sliced
250 ml (9 fl oz/1 cup) thick (double/heavy) cream
30 g (1 oz/½ cup) roughly chopped parsley

1 Add pasta to a large pan of rapidly boiling water and cook until just tender; drain.
2 Cook broccoli florets in a small pan of rapidly boiling water for 2 minutes or until tender; drain. Heat butter in a large pan. Add ham strips and stir over medium heat for 2 minutes or until ham is lightly browned.
3 Add crushed garlic, spring onion and mushrooms, stir for 2 minutes. Add drained pasta, broccoli, cream and parsley; stir for 1 minute or until heated through.

COOK'S FILE

Storage time: This recipe is best cooked just before serving.
Hint: For best flavour, use leg ham off the bone.

1

2

MACARONI WITH CHEESE SAUCE

Preparation time: 15 minutes
Total cooking time: 30 minutes
Serves 4

200 g (7 oz) macaroni
60 g (2¼ oz) butter
1 onion, chopped
2 rashers bacon, chopped
3 tablespoons plain (all-purpose) flour
625 ml (21½ fl oz/2½ cups) milk
½ teaspoon nutmeg
185 g (6½ oz/1½ cups) grated Cheddar cheese

1 Preheat oven to 180°C (350°F/Gas 4). Add macaroni to a large pan of rapidly boiling water and cook until tender; drain.

2 Heat butter in a large pan; add onion and bacon. Stir over medium heat for 4 minutes or until tender. Add flour; stir over low heat for 1 minute. Add milk gradually; stir until mixture is smooth. Stir constantly over medium heat for 4 minutes or until mixture boils and thickens. Simmer over low heat for another minute. Remove pan from heat. Stir in nutmeg.

3 Stir in pasta and 125 g (4½ oz/1 cup) of the cheese. Spoon into greased, 1.5 litre (6 cup) ovenproof dish. Sprinkle with rest of cheese and bake for 20 minutes.

1

2

1

2

3

PENNE WITH SAUTEED CHICKEN, ASPARAGUS AND GOAT'S CHEESE

Preparation time: 15 minutes
Total cooking time: 35 minutes
Serves 4

500 g (1 lb 2 oz) penne pasta
350 g (12 oz) fresh asparagus spears
1 tablespoon olive oil
2 skinless, boneless chicken breasts, cut into 3 cm (1¼ inch) cubes
1 tablespoon finely chopped thyme
250 ml (9 fl oz/1 cup) chicken stock
4 tablespoons balsamic vinegar
150 g (5½ oz) goat's cheese

1 Bring a large saucepan of salted water to the boil, add the pasta and cook for 10–12 minutes, or until al dente. Drain and keep warm.

2 Remove the woody ends from the asparagus, cut into short lengths and cook in a pan of boiling water for 3 minutes, or until just tender.

3 Heat the oil in a pan over high heat. Add the chicken and cook in batches for 5 minutes, or until browned. Return the chicken to the pan. Add the thyme and cook for 1 minute. Add the stock and vinegar and bring to the boil. Reduce the heat and simmer, stirring, for 3–4 minutes, or until the sauce has reduced slightly, then add the asparagus. Toss the pasta with the chicken in a serving bowl and crumble the cheese over the top. Season and serve.

COOK'S FILE

Variation: Feta cheese can be substituted for the goat's cheese.

1

2

3

CHICKEN CARBONARA

Preparation time: 10 minutes
Total cooking time: 20 minutes
Serves 4

350 g (12 oz) dried or 500 g (1 lb 2 oz) fresh tomato fettucine
600 g (1 lb 5 oz) chicken tenderloins
40 g (1½ oz) butter
3 eggs
300 ml (10½ fl oz) cream
50 g (1¾ oz/½ cup) freshly grated Parmesan cheese
shaved Parmesan cheese
basil leaves, to garnish

1 Bring a saucepan of salted water to the boil. Add the fettucine and cook according to the packet instructions, or until al dente. Drain and keep warm.

2 Trim and slice the tenderloins in half on the diagonal. Melt the butter in a frying pan and cook the chicken for 4–5 minutes, or until browned. Lightly beat the eggs and cream together and stir in the grated Parmesan. Season with salt to taste and stir through the chicken.

3 Combine the chicken and cream mixture with the fettucine in the frying pan. Reduce the heat and cook, stirring constantly, for 10–15 seconds, or until the sauce is slightly thickened. Do not keep on the heat too long or the eggs will set and scramble. Season with black pepper and serve, garnished with the extra Parmesan and basil leaves.

COOK'S FILE

Variation: Saffron fettucine is a delicious substitute for tomato fettucine.

SPAGHETTI WITH FRESH TOMATO SAUCE

Preparation time: 15 minutes + refrigeration
Total cooking time: 10–15 minutes
Serves 4

4 spring onions (scallions)
4 firm ripe tomatoes
8 stuffed green olives
2 tablespoons capers
2 garlic cloves, crushed
½ teaspoon dried oregano
4 tablespoons parsley, chopped
4 tablespoons olive oil
375 g (13 oz) thin spaghetti

1 Chop spring onions finely. Chop tomatoes into small pieces. Chop olives and capers. Place all ingredients, except pasta, in a bowl; mix well. Cover and refrigerate for at least 2 hours. Add pasta to a large pan of rapidly boiling water and cook until tender. Drain and return to pan.
2 Add cold sauce to hot pasta and mix well.

COOK'S FILE

Variation: Add 30 g (1 oz/½ cup) of shredded fresh basil leaves.

1

2

RAVIOLI WITH HERBS

Preparation time: 15 minutes
Total cooking time: 4 minutes
Serves 4–6

2 tablespoons olive oil
1 garlic clove, halved
800 g (1 lb 12 oz) ravioli
60 g (2¼ oz) butter, chopped
2 tablespoons chopped parsley
4 tablespoons chopped basil
2 tablespoons chopped chives

1 Combine oil and garlic in a small bowl, set aside.
2 Add ravioli to a large pan of rapidly boiling water and, cook until tender. Drain well and return to pan. Add oil to pasta; discard garlic. Add butter and herbs to ravioli, toss well.

COOK'S FILE

Variation: Use fresh coriander (cilantro) instead of parsley.

1

ORECCHIETTE WITH MUSHROOMS, PANCETTA AND SMOKED MOZZARELLA

Preparation time: 10 minutes
Cooking time: 15 minutes
Serves 4

400 g (14 oz) orecchiette
2 tablespoons olive oil
150 g (5½ oz) sliced pancetta, cut into short thin strips
200 g (7 oz) button mushrooms, sliced
2 leeks, sliced
250 ml (9 fl oz/1 cup) cream
200 g (7 oz) smoked mozzarella (mozzarella affumicata), cut into 1 cm (½ inch) cubes
8 fresh basil leaves, roughly torn

1 Cook the pasta in a large saucepan of rapidly boiling salted water according to the packet instructions until al dente.

2 Meanwhile, heat the oil in a large frying pan and sauté the pancetta, mushrooms and leek over medium–high heat for 5 minutes. Stir in the cream and season with pepper—the pancetta should provide enough salty flavour. Simmer over low heat for 5 minutes, or until the pasta is ready. Drain the pasta and stir into the frying pan. Add the mozzarella and basil and toss lightly.

COOK'S FILE

Note: If you are watching your weight, you can substitute 125 ml (4 fl oz/½ cup) chicken stock for half of the cream. Smoked provolone can be used instead of the mozzarella, if preferred.

1

PASTA WITH BEEF RAGU

Preparation time: 10 minutes
Cooking time: 1 hour 30 minutes
Serves 4

100 g (3½ oz) streaky bacon or pancetta (not trimmed), finely chopped
1 onion, finely chopped
3 garlic cloves, crushed
1 bay leaf
800 g (1 lb 12 oz) minced (ground) lean beef
500 ml (17 fl oz/2 cups) red wine
4 tablespoons tomato paste (concentrated purée)
400 g (14 oz) tagliatelle
freshly grated parmesan, to garnish

1 Heat a large deep frying pan (preferably stainless steel or non-stick). Add the bacon or pancetta and cook over medium–high heat for 2 minutes, or until soft and just starting to brown. Add the onion, garlic and bay leaf and cook for 2 minutes, or until the onion is soft and just starting to brown.

2 Add mince and stir for about 4 minutes, or until it browns, breaking up any lumps with the back of a wooden spoon. Add the wine, tomato paste and 250 ml (9 fl oz/1 cup) water and stir well. Bring to the boil, then reduce the heat and simmer, covered, for 40 minutes. Remove the lid and cook for a further 40 minutes, or until reduced to a thick, glossy sauce.

3 About 20 minutes before the ragu is ready, bring a large saucepan of salted water the boil and cook the pasta according to the packet instructions until al dente. Drain. Serve the sauce over the pasta and garnish with a little grated parmesan.

COOK'S FILE

Note: This is a great meal to prepare ahead of time, leaving the flavours to develop overnight. Then all you have to do is reheat it in a saucepan and cook your pasta.

1

2

CREAMY GARLIC PRAWN FETTUCCINE

Preparation time: 15 minutes
Cooking time: 20 minutes
Serves 4

400 g (14 oz) fresh fettuccine
2 tomatoes (about 400 g/14 oz)
1 tablespoon olive oil
1 onion, finely chopped
3 garlic cloves, crushed
3 tablespoons white wine
300 ml (10½ fl oz) cream
1 kg (2 lb 4 oz) raw medium prawns (shrimp), peeled, deveined and tails intact
15 g (½ oz/½ cup) loosely packed roughly chopped fresh basil

1 Cook the pasta in a large saucepan of boiling salted water according to the packet instructions until al dente. Drain, then return to the pan.

2 Meanwhile, score a cross in the base of the tomatoes. Place in a heatproof bowl and cover with boiling water. Leave for 30 seconds, then transfer to cold water. Peel the skin away from the cross. Cut in half, scoop out the seeds with a teaspoon and discard. Roughly chop the flesh.
Heat the oil in a large frying pan over medium–high heat and cook the onion and garlic, stirring, for 4–5 minutes, or until the onion is soft. Add the tomato and wine and cook for 3 minutes before adding the cream. Bring to the boil, then reduce the heat to medium–low and simmer for 5 minutes, or until it slightly thickens. Stir in the prawns, then simmer for 3–4 minutes, or until the prawns turn pink and are curled and cooked through. Toss with the pasta, gently stir in the basil, season and serve immediately.

1

2

FREEFORM RICOTTA AND MUSHROOM LASAGNE

Preparation time: 15 minutes
Cooking time: 15 minutes
Serves 4

250 g (9 oz/1 cup) fresh ricotta
65 g (2¼ oz/⅔ cup) grated parmesan
3½ tablespoons olive oil
1 onion, thinly sliced
2 cloves garlic, crushed
500 g (1 lb 2 oz) Swiss brown mushrooms, sliced
300 ml (10½ fl oz) good-quality Italian tomato passata
6 sheets fresh lasagne, cut in half, then cut into 12 cm (4½ inch) squares
200 g (7 oz) baby English spinach leaves, washed

1 Mix the ricotta with half the parmesan and season well. Heat 2 tablespoons of the oil in a large frying pan, add the onion and cook for 2 minutes, or until it softens. Add the garlic and mushrooms and continue to cook for 1–2 minutes, or until the mushrooms start to soften. Add the tomato passata and cook for a further 5–6 minutes, or until the sauce starts to thicken. Season well.

2 Meanwhile, bring a deep pan of water to the boil, then add 1 tablespoon of the oil and a pinch of salt. Drop the 12 pasta squares into the boiling water and cook for 2–3 minutes, or until cooked. Drain, keeping each square separate to avoid sticking together. At the same time, put the spinach in a saucepan with just the water clinging to the leaves. Cook, covered, over medium heat for 1–2 minutes, or until the spinach has wilted.

3 To assemble, place one pasta square on each serving plate, then evenly divide the mushroom sauce among the squares. Place another pasta square on top, then spread the ricotta mixture evenly over the surface, leaving a 2 cm (¾ inch) border. Divide the spinach evenly among the four servings. Finally, place another pasta square on top, brush or drizzle with the remaining oil, then sprinkle with the remaining parmesan. Season. Serve with a green salad and crusty bread.

1

2

3

SPINACH AND RICOTTA SHELLS

Preparation time: 15 minutes
Total cooking time: 15 minutes
Serves 4

20 giant pasta shells (conchiglie)
1 tablespoon oil
2 rashers bacon, finely chopped
1 onion, finely chopped
500 g (1 lb 2 oz) English spinach, chopped
750 g (1 lb 10 oz) ricotta cheese
4 tablespoons freshly grated parmesan cheese
250 g (9 oz/1 cup) tomato pasta sauce
toasted pine nuts, optional, for serving

1 Add pasta shells to a large pan of rapidly boiling water and cook until just tender; drain.
2 Heat oil in pan; add bacon and onion. Stir over medium heat for 3 minutes or until lightly browned. Add spinach, stir over low heat until wilted. Add ricotta cheese and stir until combined.
3 Spoon mixture into pasta shells, sprinkle with parmesan cheese. Place shells on cold, lightly oiled grill (broiler) tray. Cook under medium–high heat for 3 minutes or until lightly browned and heated through.
4 Place tomato pasta sauce in small pan, stir over high heat for 1 minute or until heated through. Spoon sauce onto serving plates, top with shells. Sprinkle with pine nuts, if desired.

COOK'S FILE

Storage time: Shells can be assembled with filling several hours before required. Store, covered, in refrigerator. Grill (broil) just before serving.
Variation: Use silverbeet (Swiss chard) instead of English spinach.

1

2

3

BUTTERFLY PASTA WITH PEAS, PROSCIUTTO AND MUSHROOMS

Preparation time: 10 minutes
Total cooking time: 10–15 minutes
Serves 4

375 g (13 oz) butterfly (farfalle) pasta
60 g (2¼ oz) butter
200 g (7 oz) mushrooms, thinly sliced
1 onion, chopped
250 g (9 oz) cooked peas
3 slices prosciutto, sliced
250 ml (9 fl oz/1 cup) cream
1 egg yolk

1 Add pasta to a large pan of rapidly boiling water and cook until just tender; drain and return to pan.
2 Heat butter in a separate pan; add mushrooms and onion; stir over medium heat for 5 minutes or until tender.
3 Add peas and prosciutto to pan. Combine cream and yolk in a small jug and add to pan. Cover; simmer for 5 minutes or until heated through.
4 Mix sauce through pasta or serve sauce over top and sprinkle with parmesan cheese, if desired.

COOK'S FILE

Hint: Reserve 3 tablespoons liquid when peas are cooked. Use to thin the sauce if necessary.
Variation: Add crushed garlic when cooking onion. Sprinkle with freshly chopped mint and parsley.

1

2

3

PENNE WITH SUNDRIED TOMATOES AND LEMON

Preparation time: 10 minutes
Total cooking time: 12–15 minutes
Serves 4

250 g (9 oz) penne
3 tablespoons olive oil
3 rashers bacon, chopped
1 onion, chopped
4 tablespoons lemon juice
1 tablespoon thyme leaves
4 tablespoons chopped semi-dried (sun-blushed) tomatoes
80 g (2¾ oz/½ cup) pine nuts, toasted

1 Add pasta to a large pan of rapidly boiling water and cook until just tender; drain.

2 Heat oil in a large pan. Add bacon and onion; stir over medium heat for 4 minutes or until bacon is brown and onion has softened. Add pasta to pan with lemon juice, thyme, tomato and pine nuts. Stir over low heat for 2 minutes or until heated through.

COOK'S FILE

Note: Semi-dried tomatoes will become bitter if heated too much.

Variation: Use pancetta instead of bacon, if preferred

PESTO WITH TAGLIATELLE

Preparation time: 10 minutes
Total cooking time: 10 minutes
Serves 4

250 g (9 oz) spinach tagliatelle
100 g (3½ oz/2 cups) tightly packed basil leaves
4 garlic cloves, peeled and chopped
4 tablespoons pine nuts
100 g (3½ oz/1 cup) freshly grated parmesan cheese
185 ml (6 fl oz/¾ cup) olive oil

1 Add tagliatelle to a large pan of rapidly boiling water and cook until tender. Drain well; return to pan.

2 While pasta is cooking, place basil, garlic and pine nuts in food processor and process until finely ground. Add cheese; process until well combined.

3 With motor running, slowly pour olive oil through the feed tube. Add enough sauce to pasta to coat well. Season with salt and pepper before serving. Garnish with fresh basil leaves, if desired.

1

2

COOK'S FILE

Storage time: Cook pasta just before serving. Pesto may be made in advance and kept in refrigerator. Spoon into a jar and cover sauce with a thin layer of oil.

Variations: Add extra 3 tablespoons toasted pine nuts just before serving.

GNOCCHI WITH CREAMY GORGONZOLA AND SAGE SAUCE

Preparation time: 15 minutes
Cooking time: 20 minutes
Serves 4

2 x 500 g (1 lb 2 oz) packets purchased potato gnocchi
60 g (2¼ oz) butter
2 garlic cloves, crushed
10 g (¼ oz/½ cup) fresh small sage leaves
100 g (3½ oz) gorgonzola cheese
150 ml (5 fl oz) cream
100 g (3½ oz/1 cup) grated parmesan

1 Preheat the grill (broiler) to high. Lightly grease four 250 ml (9 fl oz/ 1 cup) heatproof gratin dishes. Cook the gnocchi in a large saucepan of rapidly boiling salted water according to the packet instructions until al dente. Lift the gnocchi out with a slotted spoon, leave to drain, then divide among the prepared dishes.

2 Melt the butter in a small saucepan over medium heat, add the garlic and sage leaves and cook for a few minutes, or until the leaves start to crispen and the garlic browns a little. Pour the sage butter evenly over the gnocchi in the gratin dishes.

3 Dot small knobs of the gorgonzola evenly among the gnocchi. Pour the cream over the top of each dish and sprinkle with the parmesan. Place the dishes under the grill (broiler) and cook until the top starts to brown and the gnocchi are heated through. Serve with a fresh green salad.

COOK'S FILE

Note: This can also be cooked in a 1 litre (4 cups) rectangular heatproof ceramic dish or round pie dish.

1

2

HAM AND CHEESE PASTA BAKE

Preparation time: 15 minutes
Cooking time: 40 minutes
Serves 4

1½ tablespoons olive oil
1 onion, finely chopped
300 g (10½ oz) leg ham, sliced 3 mm (⅛ inch) thick and cut into 5 cm (2 inch) lengths
600 ml (21 fl oz) light cream
300 g (10½ oz) cooked fresh peas or frozen peas, thawed
375 g (13 oz) conchiglione (pasta shells)
3 tablespoons roughly chopped fresh basil
250 g (9 oz/2 cups) grated low-fat mature cheddar cheese

1

1 Preheat the oven to 200°C (400°F/Gas 6) and lightly grease a 2.5 litre (10 cup) ovenproof ceramic dish. Heat 1 tablespoon of the oil in a frying pan over medium heat and cook the onion, stirring frequently for 5 minutes, or until soft. Add the remaining oil, then the ham and cook, stirring, for 1 minute. Pour the cream in to the pan, bring to the boil, then reduce the heat and simmer for 6 minutes. Add the peas and cook for a further 2–4 minutes, or until the mixture has reduced and thickened slightly Season with freshly ground black pepper.

2 Meanwhile, cook the pasta in a large saucepan of rapidly boiling salted water according to the packet instructions until al dente. Drain, and return to the pan.

3 Add the cream sauce to the pasta, then the basil and three-quarters of the cheese. Stir well and season. Transfer the mixture to the prepared dish, sprinkle on the remaining cheese and bake for 20 minutes, or until the top is golden brown.

COOK'S FILE

Preparation: Prepare up to 12 hours in advance and keep refrigerated until ready to bake.

Variation: Other pasta shapes such as spirals, farfalle, fusilli or macaroni are suitable for this dish.

Simmer the balsamic vinegar and brown sugar until it becomes syrupy.

Toss the peas, asparagus, zucchini, rocket, basil and olive oil together.

Fold one third of the lasagne sheet over the salad mix, ricotta and tomato.

FRESH VEGETABLE LASAGNE WITH ROCKET

Preparation time: 20 minutes
Total cooking time: 20 minutes
Serves 4

Balsamic syrup
4 tablespoons balsamic vinegar
1½ tablespoons soft brown sugar
150 g (5½ oz/1 cup) fresh or frozen peas
16 asparagus spears, trimmed and cut into 5 cm (2 inch) lengths
2 large zucchini (courgettes), cut into thin ribbons
2 lasagne sheets (200 g/7 oz), each sheet 24 cm x 35 cm (9½ inch x 14 inch)
100 g (3½ oz) rocket (arugula) leaves
30 g (1 oz/1 cup) basil, torn
2 tablespoons extra virgin olive oil
150 g (5½ oz/1 cup) semi-dried (sun-blushed) tomatoes
250 g (9 oz/1 cup) low-fat ricotta cheese
parmesan cheese shavings, to garnish

1 To make the syrup, put the vinegar and sugar in a small saucepan. Stir over medium heat until the sugar dissolves. Reduce the heat and simmer for 3–4 minutes, or until the sauce becomes syrupy. Take off the heat.

2 Bring a large saucepan of salted water to the boil. Blanch the peas, asparagus and zucchini in separate batches until just tender, removing each batch with a slotted spoon and refreshing in cold water. Reserve the cooking liquid and return to the boil.

3 Cook the lasagne sheets in boiling water for 1–2 minutes, until al dente. Refresh in cold water and drain well. Cut each sheet in half lengthways.

4 Toss the vegetables and the rocket with the basil and olive oil. Season.

5 To assemble, place one strip of pasta on a serving plate—one-third on the centre and two-thirds overhanging. Place a small amount of the salad on the centre third, topped with some tomato and ricotta. Season lightly and fold over one-third of the lasagne sheet. Top with another layer of salad, tomato and ricotta. Fold back the final layer of pasta. Garnish with a little salad and tomato. Repeat with the remaining pasta strips, salad, ricotta and tomato to make four individual servings. Just before serving, drizzle with the balsamic syrup and garnish with parmesan.

Stir the garlic, peas and mint into the stock and leek mixture.

Stir in the cream, nutmeg and grated Parmesan.

TAGLIATELLE WITH ASPARAGUS, PEAS AND HERB SAUCE

Preparation time: 20 minutes
Total cooking time: 25 minutes
Serves 4

375 g (13 oz) dried or 500 g (1 lb 2 oz) fresh tagliatelle
250 ml (9 fl oz/1 cup) chicken or vegetable stock
2 leeks (white part only), thinly sliced
3 garlic cloves, crushed
235 g (8½ oz/1½ cups) shelled fresh peas
1 tablespoon finely chopped mint
400 g (14 oz) asparagus spears, trimmed and cut into 5 cm (2 inch) lengths
3 tablespoons finely chopped parsley
30 g (1 oz/½ cup) shredded basil
4 tablespoons light cream
pinch nutmeg
1 tablespoon grated fresh parmesan cheese
2 tablespoons extra virgin olive oil

1 Bring a large saucepan of salted water to the boil and cook the tagliatelle until al dente. Drain well.
2 Place 125 ml (4 fl oz/½ cup) of the stock and the leek in a large, deep, frying pan. Cook over low heat, stirring often, for 4–5 minutes. Stir in the garlic, peas and mint and cook for 1 minute. Add the remaining stock and 125 ml (4 fl oz/½ cup) water and bring to the boil. Simmer for 5 minutes. Add the asparagus, parsley and basil and season well with salt and freshly ground black pepper. Simmer for a further 3–4 minutes, or until the asparagus is just tender. Gradually increase the heat to reduce the sauce to a light coating consistency, if necessary. Stir in the cream, nutmeg and parmesan and adjust the seasonings to taste.
3 Add the tagliatelle to the sauce and toss lightly to coat. Divide among individual serving bowls. Drizzle with the extra virgin olive oil. Garnish with extra grated parmesan, if desired.

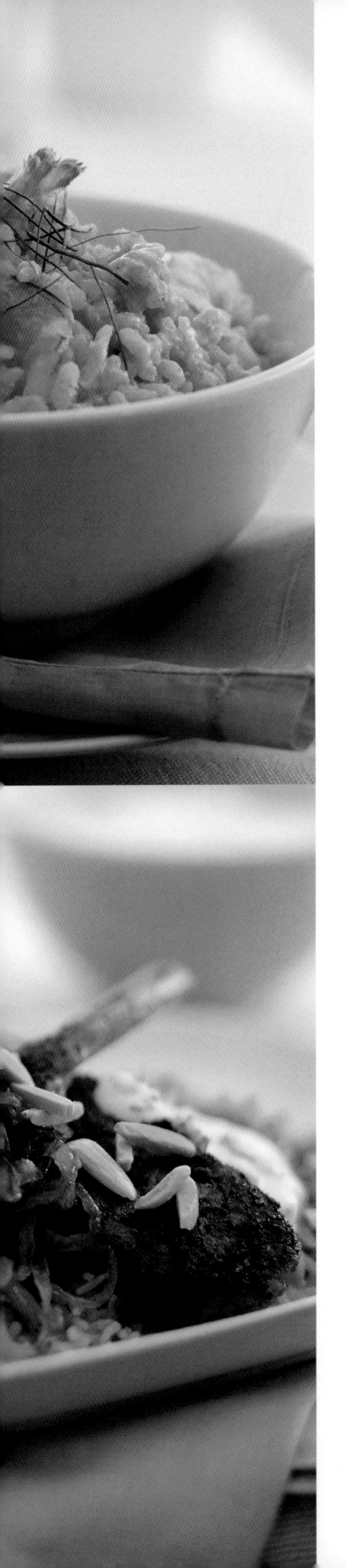

Rice

CHICKEN AND MUSHROOM PILAU

Preparation time: 15 minutes + 30 minutes standing
Cooking time: 35 minutes
Serves 4

300 g (10½ oz/1½ cups) basmati rice
2 tablespoons oil
1 large onion chopped
3–4 garlic cloves, crushed
1 tablespoon finely chopped fresh ginger
500 g (1 lb 2 oz) skinless, boneless chicken tenderloins, trimmed and cut into small pieces
300 g (10½ oz) Swiss brown mushrooms, sliced
90 g (3¼ oz/¾ cup) slivered almonds, toasted
1½–2 teaspoons garam masala, dry roasted
125 g (4½ oz/½ cup) plain yoghurt
1 tablespoon finely chopped fresh coriander (cilantro) leaves, plus extra, to garnish

1 Rinse the rice under cold water until the water runs clear. Drain and leave for 30 minutes. Heat the oil in a large saucepan over medium heat and stir in the onion, garlic and ginger. Cook, covered, for 5 minutes, or until the onion is browned. Increase the heat to high, add the chicken and cook, stirring, for 3–4 minutes, or until the chicken is lightly browned.

2 Stir in the mushrooms, almonds and garam masala. Cook, covered, for another 3 minutes, or until the mushrooms are soft. Remove the lid and cook, stirring, for 2 minutes, or until the liquid evaporates. Remove the chicken pieces from the pan.

3 Add the rice and stir for 30 seconds, or until well coated in the mushroom and onion mixture. Pour in 375 ml (13 fl oz/1½ cups) water and bring to the boil, stirring frequently to prevent the ingredients catching on the bottom of the pan. Cook for 2 minutes, or until most of the water has evaporated. Return the chicken to the pan, reduce the heat to low and steam, covered, for 15 minutes, or until the rice is cooked.

4 Meanwhile, combine the yoghurt and chopped coriander in a small bowl. Fluff the rice with a fork, then divide among serving bowls. Top with a dollop of the yoghurt mixture and garnish with coriander leaves.

1

2

FRIED RICE WITH CHINESE BARBECUE PORK

Preparation time: 15 minutes
Cooking time: 10 minutes
Serves 4

6 spring onions (scallions)
150 g snow peas (mangetaut)
200 g (7 oz) Chinese barbecue pork
3 teaspoons sesame oil
2 eggs, lightly beaten
2 cloves garlic, finely chopped
555 g (1 lb 4 oz/3 cups) cold cooked white long-grain rice
2 tablespoons soy sauce

1 Cut the spring onions and snow peas diagonally into very thin shreds. Cut the pork into thin slices.

2 Heat a wok until hot, add 1 teaspoon of the oil and swirl to coat the base. Add the egg and swirl over the base until just set. Turn over and cook for 30 seconds, or until just lightly browned, then remove from the wok. Allow the egg to cool slightly, then roll up and cut into 1 cm (½ inch) thick slices.

3 While the wok is still very hot, add the remaining oil, then the garlic, spring onion and snow peas and stir-fry for 1–2 minutes, or until slightly soft. Add the pork, rice, soy sauce and strips of omelette and toss until heated through and thoroughly combined—the soy sauce should turn the rice brown. Remove from the heat and serve immediately.

COOK'S FILE

Note: Cook 200 g (7 oz/1 cup) long-grain rice in a large saucepan of boiling water. To cool, spread the rice on a shallow tray and leave uncovered overnight in the refrigerator.

BAKED PRAWN RISOTTO WITH THAI FLAVOURS

Preparation time: 15 minutes
Cooking time: 1 hour
Serves 4

300 ml (10½ fl oz) stock (fish, chicken or vegetable)
1 stem lemongrass, bruised
4 fresh makrut (kaffir lime) leaves, finely shredded
2 tablespoons vegetable oil
1 small red onion, thinly sliced
1½–2 tablespoons good-quality Thai red curry paste
330 g (11½ oz/1½ cups) arborio rice
300 ml (10½ fl oz) coconut cream
600 g (1 lb 5 oz) raw prawns (shrimp), peeled and deveined with tails intact (see Note)

1 Preheat the oven to 180°C (350°F/ Gas 4). Pour the stock into a saucepan, add the lemongrass and half of the makrut leaves. Bring to the boil, then reduce the heat and simmer, covered, for 10 minutes.

2 Heat the oil in a flameproof casserole dish with a lid. Add the onion and cook over medium–low heat for 4–5 minutes, or until soft but not coloured. Stir in the curry paste and cook for a further minute, or until fragrant. Stir in the rice until well coated. Strain the stock into the rice then add the coconut cream. Cover and bake for 15 minutes.

3 Remove from the oven, stir the risotto well, then bake for a further 10–15 minutes. Add the prawns and mix them well into the rice—if the mixture looks a little dry add 125 ml (4 fl oz/½ cup) stock or water. Bake for a further 10–15 minutes, or until the prawns are cooked through and the rice is tender. Serve the risotto in bowls garnished with the remaining shredded makrut leaves.

COOK'S FILE

Note: To save time, you can purchase pre-peeled raw prawns with the tails intact. You will need 300 g (10½ oz), the shells make up roughly half the weight of the prawns.

Variation: You can vary the flavours of this risotto by using a green curry paste and/or a variety of seafood (e. g. lobster, calamari, scallops).

1

2

MADRAS LAMB PILAU

Preparation time: 15 minutes + 5 minutes marinating
Cooking time: 35 minutes
Serves 4

3 tablespoons oil
2 onions, thinly sliced
250 g (9 oz/1 cup) plain yoghurt
3 tablespoons good-quality Madras curry paste
400 g (14 oz/2 cups) basmati rice, rinsed well
8 large French-trimmed lamb cutlets
4 tablespoons chopped fresh mint
60 g (2¼ oz/½ cup) slivered almonds, lightly toasted

1 Heat 2 tablespoons of the oil in a large saucepan, add the onion and cook over medium heat for 4–5 minutes, or until soft. Remove half with a slotted spoon, set aside and keep warm. Add 200 g (7 oz) of the yoghurt and 2 tablespoons of the paste to the pan. Cook, stirring for 2 minutes. Stir in the rice until well coated. Pour in 500 ml (17 fl oz/2 cups) water, bring to the boil, then reduce the heat to medium–low and cook for 15–20 minutes, or until all the water has been absorbed and the rice is tender.

2 Meanwhile, smear the cutlets with the remaining curry paste and marinate for 5 minutes. Heat the remaining oil in a frying pan over high heat, then cook the cutlets for 3–4 minutes on each side, or until cooked to your liking. Remove from the heat, cover with foil and allow to rest. Combine the remaining yoghurt with 1 tablespoon of the mint.

3 To serve, stir the remaining mint through the rice, season, then divide among four serving plates. Top with the remaining onions, the lamb and the almonds. Serve with a dollop of the minted yoghurt on the side.

1

2

SPANISH SAFFRON CHICKEN AND RICE

Preparation time: 10 minutes
Cooking time: 1 hour
Serves 4

3 tablespoons olive oil
4 chicken thighs and 6 drumsticks
1 large red onion, finely chopped
1 large green capsicum (pepper), two thirds diced and one third thinly sliced
3 teaspoons sweet paprika
400 g (14 oz) tin diced tomatoes

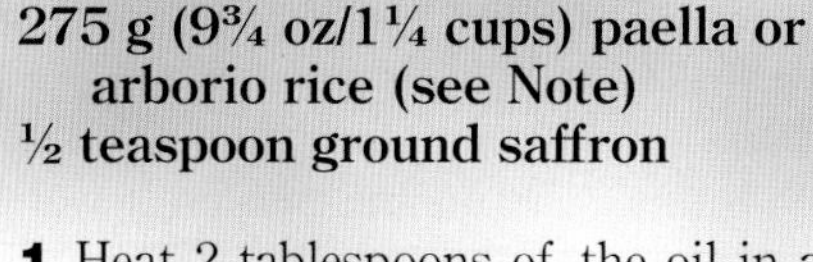

275 g (9¾ oz/1¼ cups) paella or arborio rice (see Note)
½ teaspoon ground saffron

1 Heat 2 tablespoons of the oil in a large deep frying pan over high heat. Season the chicken pieces well and brown in batches. Remove the chicken from the pan.
2 Reduce the pan to medium heat and add the remaining oil. Add the onion and the diced capsicum and cook gently for 5 minutes. Stir in the paprika and cook for 30 seconds. Add the tomato and simmer for 1–3 minutes, or until it thickens.
3 Stir in 875 ml (30 fl oz/3½ cups) boiling water to the pan, then add the rice and saffron. Return the chicken to the pan and stir to combine. Season to taste. Bring to the boil, then cover, reduce the heat to medium–low and simmer for 20–30 minutes, or until all the liquid has been absorbed and the chicken is tender. Stir in the sliced capsicum, then allow to stand, covered, for 3–4 minutes before serving.

COOK'S FILE

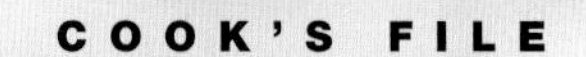

Note: Paella rice is a medium round grain from Spain. Calasparra is the most commonly available variety and can be purchased from fine food stores or Spanish delicatessens.

1

2

ONION AND PARMESAN PILAF

Preparation time: 5 minutes
Total cooking time: 20 minutes
Serves 6

60 g (2¼ oz) butter
3 onions, sliced
2 garlic cloves, crushed
200 g (7 oz/2 cups) basmati rice
1.25 litres (40 fl oz/5 cups) vegetable stock
235 g (8½ oz/1½ cups) shelled peas
50 g (1¾ oz/½ cup) grated parmesan cheese
30 g (1 oz/½ cup) chopped parsley

1 Melt butter in large pan, add onion and garlic and stir over low heat for 5 minutes, or until soft and golden.
2 Add rice and stock, bring to the boil; stir once. Reduce heat to low, simmer for 5 minutes, or until almost all the liquid has been absorbed.
3 Add peas, stir until combined. Cover pan, cook over very low heat for another 10 minutes or until rice is tender. Stir in parmesan cheese and parsley and serve immediately.

COOK'S FILE

Hint: Serve as a side dish with a barbecued chicken.
Note: Basmati rice is a fragrant rice available from supermarkets and delicatessens.

1

2

CHICKEN AND RICE WITH GREEN CAPSICUM AND TOMATOES

Preparation time: 15 minutes
Total cooking time: 1 hour
Serves 4–6

1½ tablespoons olive oil
1.2 kg (2 lb 11 oz) chicken pieces
1 onion, finely chopped
2 green capsicums (peppers), diced
3 garlic cloves, crushed
2 tablespoons paprika
300 g (10½ oz/1½ cups) long- or medium-grain rice
2 x 425 g (15 oz) tins diced tomatoes

1 Heat the oil in a large saucepan over high heat, add the chicken, skin-side down, and cook for 4 minutes each side, or until well browned. Drain the chicken on paper towels. Pour all but 1½ tablespoons of fat from the pan.

2 Reduce the heat to medium, add the onion and capsicum and cook for about 3–4 minutes, or until soft. Add the garlic, paprika and rice, and cook for a further 1 minute.

3 Add tomatoes and 560 ml (19¼ fl oz/2¼ cups) water, scraping any browned bits off the pan with a wooden spoon. Return the chicken to the pan and bring to the boil. Reduce the heat and simmer, covered, for 50 minutes, stirring occasionally to prevent sticking. Season and serve.

1

2

3

BAKED CHICKEN AND LEEK RISOTTO

Preparation time: 10 minutes
Total cooking time: 40 minutes
Serves 4–6

60 g (2¼ oz) butter
1 leek, thinly sliced
2 skinless, boneless chicken breasts, cut into 2 cm (¾ inch) cubes
440 g (15½ oz/2 cups) arborio rice (see Note)
3 tablespoons white wine
1.25 litres (5 cups) chicken stock
4 tablespoons freshly grated parmesan cheese, plus extra to serve
2 tablespoons thyme leaves
thyme leaves, to garnish

1 Preheat the oven to 150°C (300°F/ Gas 2) and place a 5 litre (20 cup) ovenproof dish with a lid in the oven to warm. Heat the butter in a saucepan over medium heat, add the leek and cook for 2 minutes, or until soft.

2 Add the chicken and cook, stirring, for 2–3 minutes, or until it colours. Add the rice and stir so that it is well coated with butter. Cook for 1 minute.

3 Add the wine and stock and bring to the boil. Pour the mixture into the warm ovenproof dish and cover. Place in the oven and cook for 30 minutes, stirring halfway through. Remove from the oven and stir through the Parmesan and thyme leaves. Season to taste. Sprinkle with extra thyme leaves and extra Parmesan and serve.

COOK'S FILE

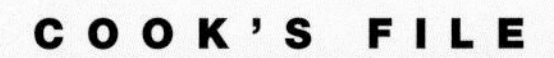

Note: Arborio rice is a special short-grain rice for making risotto.

1

2

3

Grills and barbecues

SWORDFISH SKEWERS WITH WHITE BEAN PUREE

Preparation time: 25 minutes + 30 minutes soaking + 30 minutes marinating
Total cooking time: 20 minutes
Serves 4

1 kg (2 lb 4 oz) swordfish steaks, cut into 3 cm (1¼ inch) cubes
1 tablespoon olive oil
2 tablespoons lemon juice
1 garlic clove, crushed
1 tablespoon chopped rosemary
1 tablespoon chopped thyme
2 tablespoons chopped flat-leaf (Italian) parsley

White Bean Purée
2 x 400 g (14 oz) tins cannellini beans
375 ml (13 fl oz/1½ cups) chicken stock
2 bay leaves
2 garlic cloves, crushed
1 teaspoon chopped thyme
½ teaspoon finely grated lemon zest
3 tablespoons extra virgin olive oil

1 Soak eight wooden skewers in water for at least 30 minutes. Thread the swordfish cubes onto the skewers. Place in a large non-metallic dish and pour on the combined olive oil, lemon juice, garlic, rosemary and thyme. Season well. Cover with plastic wrap and refrigerate for at least 30 minutes.
2 Meanwhile, to make the white bean purée, wash the beans in a colander and place in a large saucepan. Add the chicken stock, bay leaves and 125 ml (4 fl oz/½ cup) water. Bring to the boil, then reduce the heat and simmer for 10 minutes. Remove from the heat and drain well, reserving 2 tablespoons of the liquid.
3 Place the beans and the reserved liquid in a food processor or blender with the garlic, thyme and lemon zest. Season with salt and pepper and process until smooth. with the motor running, gradually pour in the olive oil in a thin stream. Continue processing until well combined, then keep warm.
4 Heat a chargrill (griddle) or hot plate until very hot. Cook the skewers, turning regularly and basting with any leftover marinade, for 3–4 minutes, or until cooked through and golden. Serve the skewers warm, sprinkled with parsley and a spoonful of white bean purée on the side.

Drain the beans over a heatproof bowl and reserve some of the liquid.

Process the beans, garlic, thyme and lemon zest, then the oil, in a food processor.

Chargrill the swordfish skewers until cooked through and golden.

PIRI-PIRI CHICKEN

Preparation time: 5 minutes + 1 hour marinating
Total cooking time: 1 hour
Serves 4

6 bird's eye chillies, finely chopped, with seeds
1 teaspoon coarse salt
125 ml (4 fl oz/½ cup) olive oil
185 ml (6 fl oz/¾ cup) cider vinegar
1 garlic clove, crushed
4 chicken Maryland (leg quarter) pieces
4 lemon wedges

1 Combine the chilli, salt, olive oil, vinegar and garlic in a jar. Seal and shake well to combine.

2 Place the chicken pieces in a shallow dish and pour on the marinade. Cover and marinate for 1 hour, or overnight if time permits.

3 Cook the chicken on a hot barbecue or chargrill pan (griddle), as close to the flame as possible, basting regularly with the marinade, for 50–60 minutes, or until the chicken is cooked through and the skin begins to crisp. Serve with lemon wedges, corn cobs and steamed green beans.

COOK'S FILE

Note: Any chicken cut that is still on the bone can be used in this recipe. Piri-piri is also excellent for barbecuing prawns (shrimp). Deseed the chillies for a milder tasting dish.

1

2

3

1

2

LAMB CUTLETS WITH MINT GREMOLATA

Preparation time: 15 minutes
Cooking time: 10 minutes
Serves 4

4 tablespoons fresh mint leaves
1 tablespoon fresh flat-leaf (Italian) parsley
2 garlic cloves
1½ tablespoons lemon rind (white pith removed), cut into thin strips
2 tablespoons extra virgin olive oil
8 French-trimmed lamb cutlets
2 carrots
2 zucchini (courgettes)
1 tablespoon lemon juice

1 To make the gremolata, finely chop the mint, parsley, garlic and lemon strips, then combine well.

2 Heat a chargrill pan (griddle) or barbecue plate to very hot. Lightly brush with 1 tablespoon of the oil. Cook the cutlets over medium heat for 2 minutes on each side, or until cooked to your liking. Remove the cutlets and cover to keep warm.

3 Trim the ends from the carrots and zucchini and, using a sharp vegetable peeler, peel the vegetables lengthways into ribbons. Heat remaining oil in a large saucepan, add vegetables and toss over medium heat for 3–5 minutes, or until sautéed but tender.

4 Divide the cutlets among the serving plates, sprinkle the cutlets with the gremolata and drizzle with the lemon juice. Serve with the vegetable ribbons.

COOK'S FILE

Hint: Use a vegetable peeler to remove the rind from the lemon.

BARBECUED STEAK WITH CARAMELIZED BALSAMIC ONIONS AND MUSTARD CREME FRAICHE

Preparation time: 15 minutes
Cooking time: 35 minutes
Serves 4

1½ tablespoons wholegrain mustard
200 g (7 oz) crème fraîche
1 red capsicum (pepper), deseeded and quartered
1 yellow capsicum (pepper) deseeded and quartered
2 zucchini (courgettes), trimmed and sliced lengthways into strips
2 tablespoons oil
2 large red onions, thinly sliced
4 rump steaks (about 200 g/ 7 oz each)
2 tablespoons soft brown sugar
3 tablespoons balsamic vinegar

1 Preheat a flat barbecue hotplate or large chargrill pan (griddle) to hot. Combine the mustard and crème fraîche in a bowl. Season. Cover and set aside.

2 Brush the capsicum and zucchini with 1 tablespoon of the oil. Cook the capsicum, turning regularly, on the hotplate for 5 minutes, or until tender and slightly charred. Remove and cover with foil. Repeat with the zucchini, also cooking for 5 minutes.

3 Heat the remaining oil on the hotplate, then cook the onion, turning occasionally, for 5–10 minutes, or until softened. When nearly soft, push to the side of the hotplate, then add the steaks and cook on each side for 3–4 minutes (medium–rare), or until cooked to your liking. Remove the steaks, cover with foil and allow to rest. Spread the onion over the hotplate once again, reduce the heat, sprinkle with sugar and cook for 1–2 minutes, or until the sugar has dissolved and the onion appears glossy. Add the vinegar, stirring continuously for 1–2 minutes or until it is absorbed. Remove at once.

4 Peel the skin off the capsicum, then divide among four serving plates with the zucchini. Place the steaks on top, season and top with the balsamic onions. Serve with the mustard crème fraîche and a mixed leaf salad.

1

1

TRADITIONAL GARLIC PRAWNS

Preparation time: 20 minutes
Total cooking time: 5 minutes
Serves 4

250 ml (9 fl oz/1 cup) oil
60 g (2¼ oz) butter, cut in 4 even-sized cubes
8 garlic cloves, peeled
2 small red chillies, deseeded and finely sliced
20 medium raw king prawns (shrimp), peeled, tails intact
2 tablespoons chopped parsley
baguette, for serving

1 Divide oil among 4 fireproof dishes. Add 1 cube of butter to each dish. Prepare and heat barbecue.

2 Remove veins from prawns. Crush 2 cloves of garlic into each dish and divide chilli among the 4 dishes. Heat dishes on a barbecue flatplate until butter is very hot and bubbling. Add 5 prawns to each dish and cook for 3–4 minutes or until prawns are pink and cooked through. Sprinkle with parsley. Serve with the baguette.

COOK'S FILE

Variation: Prawns can be cooked in a pan on a hotplate. Heat oil with butter, garlic and chilli in a medium pan. When bubbling, add prawns and cook until pink. Preheat oven to 210°C (415°F/Gas 6–7). Heat 4 heatproof serving dishes in oven. Remove dishes from oven and place 5 prawns in each dish. Spoon some oil into each dish.

CHAR-GRILLED BABY OCTOPUS

Preparation time: 20 minutes + marinating
Total cooking time: 5 minutes
Serves 4

500 g (1 lb 2 oz) baby octopus
125 ml (4 fl oz/½ cup) olive oil
2 tablespoons lemon juice
2 tablespoons finely chopped coriander (cilantro)
1 tablespoon chilli sauce

1 Using a sharp knife, cut head from octopus; remove gut from inside. Push the beak up and out of lower section and discard. Wash octopus thoroughly and dry on paper towels.

2 Place remaining ingredients in a bowl and whisk until well combined. Add octopus to the bowl and stir well. Cover and refrigerate for 2 hours or overnight. Stir occasionally.

3 Heat grill (broiler) or barbecue plate; brush with oil to prevent sticking. Drain octopus; reserve marinade. Cook octopus for 2–3 minutes on one side; turn over and continue cooking for another 2–3 minutes. Brush with reserved marinade while cooking. Serve immediately. Garnish with coriander, if desired.

COOK'S FILE

Hint: Octopus will toughen if it is overcooked.

1

2

CHICKEN WITH LEMON AND BASIL SAUCE

Preparation time: 10 minutes
Total cooking time: 10 minutes
Serves 4

55 g (2 oz/⅔ cup) fresh breadcrumbs
3 tablespoons olive oil
3 tablespoons lemon juice
3 tablespoons chopped basil
3 garlic cloves, crushed
1 teaspoon sugar
8 skinless, boneless chicken thighs
1 tablespoon olive oil, extra

1 Place breadcrumbs in a food processor or blender. Add oil, lemon juice, basil, garlic and sugar. Blend for 20 seconds or until smooth. Transfer to medium pan and stir gently over low heat 2 minutes or until heated through. Serve with chicken.

2 Trim chicken of excess fat and sinew. Place on cold, lightly oiled grill (broiler) tray. Brush chicken with oil and cook under medium–high heat 5 minutes each side or until tender. Serve with sauce. Garnish with basil.

COOK'S FILE

Storage time: Sauce can be made several hours before required. Store, with plastic wrap pressed down over surface of sauce, in refrigerator.

Variation: Chicken can be fried or baked instead of grilled (broiled).

SATAY CHICKEN

Preparation time: 15 minutes
Total cooking time: 10–15 minutes
Serves 4

750 g (1 lb 10 oz) skinless, boneless chicken thighs
1 tablespoon oil
1 onion, chopped
125 g (4½ oz/½ cup) crunchy peanut butter
4 tablespoons chicken stock
2 garlic cloves, crushed
2 tablespoons fruit chutney
3 teaspoons red curry paste
2 teaspoons soy sauce

1 Trim chicken thigh fillets of excess fat and sinew. Cut chicken into 2.5 cm (1 inch) cubes. Soak wooden skewers in water.

2 Heat oil in pan; add onion and stir until soft. Transfer to food processor or blender. Add remaining ingredients. Process for 1 minute or until smooth.

3 Thread chicken onto skewers. Place skewers on cold, lightly oiled grill (broiler) tray; brush with peanut mixture. Cook under high heat for 5 minutes on each side or until tender, brushing with peanut mixture several times during cooking. Place remaining peanut mixture in a small pan, stir over medium heat for 3–5 minutes or until boiling. Serve with chicken skewers.

COOK'S FILE

Storage time: Chicken can be marinated in refrigerator overnight.

1

SUMAC-CRUSTED LAMB FILLETS WITH BABA GANOUJ

Preparation time: 15 minutes
Cooking time: 25 minutes
Serves 4

2 tablespoons olive oil
750 g (1 lb 10 oz) small new potatoes
2–3 garlic cloves, crushed
3 tablespoons lemon juice
1 red capsicum (pepper), deseeded and quartered lengthways
4 lamb backstraps (about 200 g/ 7 oz each)
1 tablespoon sumac (see Note)
3 tablespoons chopped fresh flat-leaf (Italian) parsley
250 g (9 oz) good-quality baba ganouj

1 Heat the oil in a saucepan big enough to hold the potatoes in one layer. Add the potatoes and garlic, and cook, turning frequently, for 3–5 minutes, or until brown all over. When golden, add the lemon juice and reduce the heat to medium–low. Gently simmer, covered, for 15–20 minutes, or until tender; stir occasionally to prevent sticking. Remove from the heat. Season well.

2 Meanwhile, lightly oil a chargrill pan (griddle) or barbecue plate and heat to very hot. Cook the capsicum pieces skin-side-down for 1–2 minutes, or until the skin starts to blister and turn black. Cook the other side for 1–2 minutes. Remove from the heat, then place in a plastic bag or bowl covered with plastic wrap. Set aside.

3 Coat the lamb with sumac. Cook on the chargrill pan for 4–5 minutes on each side, or until cooked to your liking. Remove from the heat, cover with foil and rest. Remove the skin from the capsicum and slice the quarters into thin strips.

4 Stir the parsley through the potatoes. Divide the baba ganouj among four plates. Cut the lamb into 1 cm (½ inch) slices on the diagonal and arrange on top of the baba ganouj with the capsicum strips. Serve with the potatoes and a green salad.

COOK'S FILE

Note: Sumac is available from Middle Eastern grocery stores and some gourmet food retailers. If unavailable, use the same amount of ground cumin.

1

2

BARBECUED CHERMOULA PRAWNS

Preparation time: 15 minutes + 10 minutes standing
Cooking time: 10 minutes
Serves 4

1 kg (2 lb 4 oz) raw medium prawns (shrimp)
3 teaspoons hot paprika
2 teaspoons ground cumin
30 g (1 oz/1 cup) firmly packed fresh flat-leaf (Italian) parsley
15 g (½ oz/½ cup) firmly packed fresh coriander (cilantro) leaves
100 ml (3½ fl oz) lemon juice
145 ml (4¾ fl oz) olive oil
280 g (10 oz/1½ cups) couscous
1 tablespoon grated lemon zest
lemon wedges, to serve

1 Peel prawns, leaving the tails intact. Gently pull out the dark vein from the backs, starting at the head end. Place the prawns in a large bowl. Dry-fry the paprika and cumin in a frying pan for about 1 minute, or until fragrant. Remove from the heat.

2 Blend or process the spices, parsley, coriander, lemon juice and 125 ml (4 fl oz/½ cup) of the oil until finely chopped. Add a little salt and pepper. Pour over the prawns and mix well, then cover with plastic wrap and refrigerate for 10 minutes. Heat a chargrill pan (griddle) or barbecue plate to hot.

3 Meanwhile, to cook the couscous, bring 250 ml (9 fl oz/1 cup) water to the boil in a saucepan, then stir in the couscous, lemon zest, the remaining oil and ¼ teaspoon salt. Remove from the heat, cover and leave for 5 minutes. Fluff the couscous with a fork, adding a little extra olive oil if needed.

4 Cook the prawns on the chargrill pan for about 3–4 minutes, or until cooked through, turning and brushing with extra marinade while cooking (take care not to overcook). Serve the prawns on a bed of couscous, with a wedge of lemon.

1

1

2

TANDOORI CHICKEN AND VEGETABLE SKEWERS

Preparation time: 15 minutes
Total cooking time: 10 minutes
Serves 4

250 g (9 oz/1 cup) plain yoghurt
2 garlic cloves, crushed
2 teaspoons grated fresh ginger
2 teaspoons ground turmeric
2 teaspoons garam masala
6 skinless, boneless chicken thighs, cut into 4 cm (1½ inch) cubes
1 red capsicum (pepper), cut into 2.5 cm (1 inch) squares
1 onion, cut into thin wedges

1 Combine yoghurt in a small bowl with garlic, ginger, turmeric and garam masala. Set aside.
2 Thread chicken, capsicum and onion alternately onto soaked skewers. Brush yoghurt mixture lightly over skewers.
3 Place skewers on cold, lightly oiled grill (broiler) tray and cook, brushing with yoghurt mixture occasionally, under high heat for 5 minutes. Turn and cook, brushing again with yoghurt mixture, for 5 minutes or until chicken is tender. Serve with saffron rice, if desired.

COOK'S FILE

Storage time: Skewers can be prepared a day ahead. Store, covered, in refrigerator. Cook just before serving.

PORK STEAKS WITH ORANGE ROSEMARY SAUCE

Preparation time: 10 minutes
Total cooking time: 10 minutes
Serves 4

1 teaspoon grated orange zest
2 tablespoons orange juice
2 tablespoons olive oil
1 tablespoon seeded mustard
2 teaspoons chopped rosemary
2 teaspoons Worcestershire sauce
4 pork butterfly steaks

1 In a small bowl, combine orange zest and juice, oil, mustard, rosemary and Worcestershire sauce.

2 Place pork on lightly oiled grill (broiler) tray; brush with orange mixture. Cook under high heat for 5 minutes on each side or until cooked through, turning once. Brush medallions occasionally with orange mixture during cooking. Serve with fine strips of orange zest and salad greens, if desired.

1

COOK'S FILE

Storage time: Orange mixture can be made several hours in advance. Store, covered, in refrigerator. Cook medallions just before serving.
Variation: Pork schnitzels are also suitable for this recipe.

PAPRIKA LAMB KEBABS WITH SKORDALIA

Preparation time: 15 minutes + 30 minutes soaking
Cooking time: 30 minutes
Serves 4

1 kg (2 lb 4 oz) lamb backstraps, cut into 2 cm (¾ inch) cubes
1 tablespoon sweet paprika
1 tablespoon hot paprika
125 ml (4 fl oz/½ cup) lemon juice
125 ml (4 fl oz/½ cup) olive oil
3 large (750 g/1 lb 10 oz) floury potatoes (e.g. russet), cut into large cubes
3–4 garlic cloves, crushed with a pinch of salt
300 g (6 cups) English spinach leaves
lemon wedges, to serve

1 Soak 12 wooden skewers in water for 30 minutes to prevent them burning during cooking. Thread six lamb cubes onto each skewer, then place in a non-metallic rectangular dish large enough to hold all of the skewers in one layer.

2 To make the marinade, combine both the paprikas, 4 tablespoons of the lemon juice and 3 tablespoons of the oil in a small non-metallic jug. Pour over the skewers, turning to ensure they are well coated. Season with pepper. Cover and refrigerate while making the skordalia.

3 To make the skordalia, boil the potatoes for 20 minutes, or until tender. Drain and place the potatoes, garlic and 1 tablespoon of the lemon juice in a food processor. With the motor running, slowly add the remaining oil in a thin stream and continue blending for 30–60 seconds, or until all the oil is incorporated—avoid overprocessing as it will become gluey. Season. Set aside to serve at room temperature.

4 Preheat a chargrill pan (griddle) or barbecue plate and brush with oil. Add the skewers and chargrill for 3–4 minutes on each side for medium–rare, or 5–6 minutes for well done.

5 Meanwhile, wash the spinach and add to a saucepan with just the water clinging to the leaves. Cook, covered, over medium heat for 1–2 minutes, or until the spinach has wilted. Remove from the heat and stir in the remaining lemon juice. Serve the kebabs immediately with the skordalia, spinach and lemon wedges.

COOK'S FILE

Variation: Alternate cherry tomatoes, onion wedges or pieces of capsicum (pepper) and zucchini (courgette) with the lamb cubes.

CAJUN CHICKEN WITH FRESH TOMATO AND CORN SALSA

Preparation time: 15 minutes
Cooking time: 15 minutes
Serves 4

2 corn cobs
2 vine-ripened tomatoes, diced
1 Lebanese (short) cucumber, diced
2 tablespoons chopped fresh coriander (cilantro) leaves
4 skinless, boneless chicken breasts (about 200 g/ 7 oz each)
3 tablespoons cajun seasoning
2 tablespoons lime juice
lime wedges, to serve

1 Cook the corn cobs in a saucepan of boiling water for 5 minutes, or until tender. Remove the kernels using a sharp knife and place in a bowl with the tomato, cucumber and coriander. Season and mix well.

2 Heat a chargrill pan (griddle) or barbecue plate to medium heat and brush lightly with oil. Pound each chicken breast between two sheets of plastic wrap with a mallet or rolling pin until 2 cm (¾ inch) thick. Lightly coat the chicken with the cajun seasoning and shake off any excess. Cook for 5 minutes on each side, or until just cooked through.

3 Just before serving stir lime juice into the salsa. Place a chicken breast on each serving plate and spoon salsa on the side. Serve with lime wedges, a green salad and crusty bread.

1

2

ROSEMARY AND RED WINE STEAKS WITH BARBECUED VEGETABLES

Preparation time: 15 minutes + 25 minutes marinating
Cooking time: 45 minutes
Serves 4

12 small new potatoes
3 tablespoons olive oil
1 tablespoon finely chopped fresh rosemary
6 garlic cloves, sliced
sea salt flakes, to season
4 large, thick field mushrooms
12 asparagus spears
250 ml (9 fl oz/1 cup) red wine
4 scotch fillet steaks (about 260 g/9¼ oz each)

1 Heat a barbecue plate or chargrill pan (griddle) to hot. Toss the potatoes with 1 tablespoon of the oil, half the rosemary and half the garlic, and season with sea salt flakes. Divide potatoes among four large sheets of foil (three potatoes per sheet) and wrap into neat packages, sealing firmly around the edges. Place on the barbecue and cook, turning frequently for about 30–40 minutes, or until the potatoes are tender.

2 Meanwhile, brush the mushrooms and asparagus with a little of the remaining oil and set aside.

3 Combine the red wine with the remaining oil, rosemary and garlic in a non-metallic dish. Season with lots of freshly ground black pepper. Add the steaks and turn to coat well in the marinade. Allow to marinate for 25 minutes, then drain.

4 Place the steaks on the barbecue with the mushrooms and cook for 4 minutes each side, or until cooked to your liking (this will depend on the thickness of your steak). Transfer the steaks and mushrooms to a plate, cover lightly and allow to rest. Add the asparagus to the barbecue, turning regularly for about 2 minutes, or until tender. By this stage your potatoes should be cooked—open the foil and pierce with a skewer to check that they are tender–soft, and ready to eat. Season with salt and pepper. Serve a steak per person, accompanied by a mushroom, three asparagus spears and a potato package.

1

2

SESAME CHICKEN KEBABS

Preparation time: 10 minutes + 30 minutes soaking + 2 hours marinating
Total cooking time: 10 minutes
Serves 4

3 tablespoons oil
2 tablespoons soy sauce
2 tablespoons honey
1 tablespoon grated fresh ginger
1 tablespoon sesame oil
4 large skinless, boneless chicken breasts, cut into 2 cm (¾ inch) cubes
8 spring onions (scallions), cut into 2 cm (¾ inch) lengths
1 tablespoon toasted sesame seeds

1 Soak 12 wooden skewers in water for 30 minutes to prevent burning. To make the marinade, whisk together the oil, soy sauce, honey, ginger and sesame oil. Thread the chicken and spring onion alternately onto the skewers and place in a glass dish. Pour the marinade over the skewers, cover and refrigerate for 2 hours, or overnight if time permits.

2 Place the skewers on a grill (broiler) tray and place under a hot grill (broiler). Baste with the marinade and cook, turning once, for 10 minutes, or until cooked through. Sprinkle with the toasted sesame seeds. Serve with chargrilled vegetables, if desired.

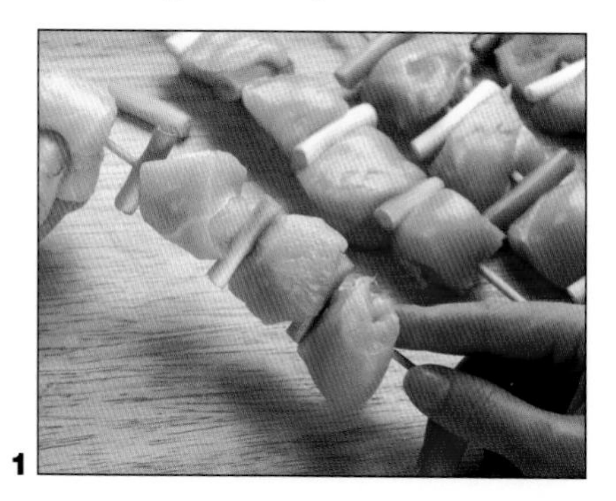
1

2

COOK'S FILE

Note: These kebabs can also be barbecued.
Hint: To toast sesame seeds, place in a dry pan and shake over moderate heat until the seeds are golden.

FILLET STEAK WITH PEPPER CHEESE SAUCE

Preparation time: 5 minutes
Total cooking time: 5–10 minutes
Serves 4

4 large beef fillet steaks

Pepper cheese sauce
2 tablespoons oil
1 small leek, thinly sliced or 1 onion, thinly sliced
250 ml (9 fl oz/1 cup) chicken stock
125 g (4½ oz) pepper cheese, cut in small cubes

1 Place steaks on cold, lightly oiled grill (broiler) tray. Cook under high heat for 2 minutes each side to seal, turning once. For rare meat, cook for another minute each side. For medium and well-done meat, lower grill (broiler) tray or reduce heat. Cook for another 2–3 minutes each side for medium and 4–6 minutes each side for well-done.

2 To make pepper cheese sauce, heat oil in a medium pan, add leek or onion. Stir over medium heat for 3 minutes or until tender. Add stock and cheese, stir for 1 minute or until cheese has melted and sauce has thickened. Serve with steaks.

COOK'S FILE

Variation: This sauce is delicious with grilled lamb, pork and veal chops.

1

2

GRILLED VEGETABLES WITH ROSEMARY AND GARLIC

Preparation time: 10 minutes
Total cooking time: 15 minutes
Serves 4

2 large orange sweet potatoes
2 large red capsicums (peppers)
6 medium zucchini (courgettes), sliced in half lengthways
4 large mushroom caps

Dressing
4 tablespoons olive oil
2 tablespoons balsamic vinegar
2 tablespoons chopped rosemary
3 garlic cloves, crushed

1 Cut sweet potatoes into thick slices. Remove seeds and membrane from capsicum. Cut flesh in thick strips. Place with zucchini and mushroom caps on a cold, lightly oiled grill (broiler) tray, brush with dressing. Cook under high heat for 15 minutes or until vegetables are tender and lightly golden, turning occasionally. Brush with remaining dressing several times during cooking.

1

2 To make dressing, place oil, vinegar, rosemary, garlic, salt and pepper in a bowl; whisk to combine.

2

COOK'S FILE

Storage time: Cook vegetables just before serving. Dressing can be prepared and stored in refrigerator.

TANDOORI CHICKEN WITH CARDAMOM RICE

Preparation time: 15 minutes + 30 minutes soaking + 10 minutes marinating
Cooking time: 25 minutes
Serves 4

200 g (7 oz) plain yoghurt, plus extra for serving
3 tablespoons good-quality tandoori paste
2 tablespoons lemon juice
1 kg (2 lb 4 oz) skinless, boneless chicken breasts, cut into 3 cm (1¼ inch) cubes
1 tablespoon oil
1 onion, finely diced
300 g (10½ oz/1½ cups) long-grain rice
2 cardamom pods, bruised
750 ml (26 fl oz/3 cups) hot chicken stock
400 g (14 oz) English spinach leaves

1 Soak eight wooden skewers in water for 30 minutes to prevent them burning during cooking. Combine the yoghurt, tandoori paste and lemon juice in a non-metallic dish. Add the chicken and coat well, then cover and marinate for at least 10 minutes.

2 Meanwhile, heat the oil in a saucepan. Add the onion and cook for 3 minutes, then add the rice and cardamom pods. Cook, stirring often, for 3–5 minutes, or until the rice is slightly opaque. Add the stock and bring to the boil. Reduce the heat to low, cover and cook, without removing the lid, for 15 minutes.

3 Heat a barbecue plate or grill (broiler) to very hot. Thread the chicken cubes onto the skewers, leaving the bottom quarter of the skewers empty. Cook on each side for 4–5 minutes, or until cooked through.

4 Wash the spinach and place in a large saucepan with just the water clinging to the leaves. Cook, covered, over medium heat for 1–2 minutes, or until the spinach has wilted. Uncover the rice, fluff with a fork and serve with the spinach, chicken and extra yoghurt.

COOK'S FILE

Ahead of time: Marinate the chicken for up to 48 hours in advance.

1

BARBECUED ASIAN PORK RIBS WITH SPRING ONION RICE

Preparation time: 15 minutes + 10 minutes marinating
Cooking time: 40 minutes
Serves 4

1 kg (2 lb 4 oz) American-style pork ribs, cut into sections of 4–5 ribs
3 tablespoons hoisin sauce
1 tablespoons Chinese rice wine or dry sherry
3 tablespoons soy sauce
2 garlic cloves, chopped
2 tablespoons oil
3 spring onions (scallions), finely chopped
1 tablespoon grated fresh ginger
250 g (9 oz/1¼ cups) jasmine rice
600 g (1 lb 5 oz) baby bok choy (pok choy), leaves separated

1 Place the ribs in a non-metallic bowl. Combine the hoisin sauce, rice wine, soy sauce, garlic, 1 tablespoon of the oil, 2 tablespoons of the spring onion and half the ginger. Pour onto the ribs and mix to coat. Marinate for at least 10 minutes, or overnight in the refrigerator.
2 Bring a large saucepan of water to the boil. Add the rice and cook for 12 minutes, stirring occasionally. Drain well.
3 Heat the remaining oil in a small saucepan over medium–low heat. When the oil is warm but not smoking, remove the pan from the heat and add the remaining spring onion and ginger. Season with ¼ teaspoon salt, stirring quickly to combine. Stir this mixture through the rice.
4 Preheat a chargrill pan (griddle) or barbecue plate and brush with oil. Remove the ribs from the marinade with tongs and reserve the marinade. Cook the ribs in batches, if necessary, for 8–10 minutes on each side, or until cooked through, basting with the marinade during cooking.
5 Five minutes before the ribs are cooked, place the reserved marinade in a saucepan and bring to the boil (add 4 tablespoons water if there is not much liquid). Boil for 2 minutes, then add the bok choy, stirring to coat. Cook, covered, for 1–2 minutes, or until just wilted. Serve the ribs with the rice and bok choy, and drizzle with the marinade.

1

2

1

GLAZED GRILLED FISH

Preparation time: 10 minutes + marinating
Total cooking time: 8 minutes
Serves 4

2 tablespoons olive oil
2 tablespoons lemon juice
2 tablespoons fruit chutney
1 tablespoon honey
1 tablespoon chopped coriander (cilantro)
2 garlic cloves, crushed
4 snapper fillets

1 Combine oil, lemon juice, fruit chutney, honey, coriander and crushed garlic in a small jug. Place fish fillets in a large non-metal dish. Pour oil mixture over fish. Cover and refrigerate for 1 hour.
2 Transfer fish fillets to cold, lightly oiled grill (broiler) tray and cook under high heat, brushing with remaining marinade occasionally, for 4 minutes each side or until tender. Serve with lemon slices, if desired.

COOK'S FILE

Storage time: The marinade can be made several hours ahead. Brush over fish and cook just before serving.
Variation: Substitute any firm-fleshed fish such as salmon or ling.

DRUMSTICKS IN TOMATO AND MANGO CHUTNEY

Preparation time: 10 minutes + 2 hours marinating
Total cooking time: 45 minutes
Serves 4

8 chicken drumsticks, scored
1 tablespoon mustard powder
2 tablespoons tomato sauce (ketchup)
1 tablespoon sweet mango chutney
1 teaspoon Worcestershire sauce
1 tablespoon dijon mustard
3 tablespoons raisins
1 tablespoon oil

1 Preheat the oven to 200°C (400°F/ Gas 6). Toss the chicken in the mustard powder and season.
2 Combine the tomato sauce, chutney, Worcestershire sauce, mustard, raisins and oil. Spoon over the chicken and toss well to coat evenly. Marinate for 2 hours, or overnight if time permits, turning halfway through.
3 Put the chicken in a shallow baking tray and bake for 45 minutes, or until the flesh pulls away from the bone.

COOK'S FILE

Serving suggestion: Serve with toasted Turkish bread and a mixture of yoghurt, cucumber and mint.

1

2

3

VEGETABLE SKEWERS WITH BASIL COUSCOUS

Preparation time: 15 minutes + 30 minutes soaking + 10 minutes standing
Cooking time: 15 minutes
Serves 4

5 thin zucchini (courgettes), cut into 2 cm (¾ inch) cubes
5 slender eggplants (aubergines), cut into 2 cm (¾ inch) cubes
12 button mushrooms, halved
2 red capsicums (peppers), cut into 1.5 cm (⅝ inch) cubes
250 g (9 oz) kefalotyri cheese, cut into 2 cm (¾ inch) thick pieces (see Note)
4 tablespoons lemon juice
2 garlic cloves, finely chopped
5 tablespoons finely chopped fresh basil
145 ml (4¾ fl oz) extra virgin olive oil
185 g (6½ oz/1 cup) couscous
1 teaspoon grated lemon zest

1 Soak 12 wooden skewers in water for 30 minutes to prevent them burning during cooking. Thread alternate pieces of vegetables and kefalotyri, starting and finishing with a piece of capsicum and using two pieces of kefalotyri per skewer. Place in a non-metallic dish large enough to hold them in one layer.
2 Combine the lemon juice, garlic, 4 tablespoons of the basil and 125 ml (4 fl oz/½ cup) of the oil in a non-metallic bowl. Season. Pour two-thirds of the marinade over the skewers, reserving the remainder. Turn the skewers to coat evenly, cover with plastic wrap and marinate for at least 5 minutes.
3 Place the couscous, lemon zest and 375 ml (13 fl oz/1½ cups) boiling water in a large heatproof bowl. Stand for 5 minutes, or until all the water has been absorbed. Add the remaining oil and basil, then fluff gently with a fork to separate the grains. Cover.
4 Meanwhile, heat a chargrill pan (griddle) or barbecue plate to medium-high. Cook the skewers, brushing often with the leftover marinade in the non-metallic dish, for 4–5 minutes on each side, or until the vegetables are cooked and the cheese browns—take care that the cheese doesn't fall apart during cooking.
5 Divide the couscous and skewers among four serving plates. Season, then drizzle with the reserved marinade to taste. Serve immediately with lemon wedges, if desired.

COOK'S FILE

Note: Kefalotyri can be found in continental delicatessens and in some larger supermarkets. If not available, use haloumi instead.

LIME AND CORIANDER CHARGRILLED CHICKEN

Preparation time: 15 minutes + 1 hour marinating
Cooking time: 15 minutes
Serves 4

3 teaspoons finely grated fresh ginger
25 g (1 oz/½ cup) chopped fresh coriander (cilantro) leaves
1½ teaspoons grated lime zest
4 tablespoons lime juice
4 skinless, boneless chicken breasts (about 750 g/ 1 lb 10 oz), trimmed
250 g (9 oz/1¼ cup) jasmine rice
2 tablespoons oil
3 zucchini (courgettes), cut into wedges
4 large flat mushrooms, stalks trimmed

1 Combine the ginger, coriander, zest and 2 tablespoons of the lime juice. Spread 2 teaspoons of this herb mixture over each fillet and season well. Marinate for 1 hour. Combine the remaining herb mixture with the remaining lime juice in a screwtop jar. Set aside until needed.

2 Bring a large saucepan of water to the boil. Add the rice and cook for 12 minutes, stirring occasionally. Drain well.

3 Meanwhile, heat a chargrill pan (griddle) or barbecue plate to medium and lightly brush with oil. Brush the zucchini and mushrooms with the remaining oil. Place the chicken on the chargrill and cook on each side for 4–5 minutes, or until cooked through. Add the vegetables during the last 5 minutes of cooking, and turn frequently until browned on the outside and just softened. Cover with foil until ready to serve.

4 Divide the rice among four serving bowls. Cut the chicken into long thick strips, then arrange on top of the rice. Shake the dressing well and drizzle over the chicken and serve with the chargrilled vegetables.

COOK'S FILE

Note: Allow chargrill pan (griddle) to heat evenly to medium heat. Do not cook on a smoking hot grill or the chicken will singe, overcooking the outside and not evenly throughout.

1

2

ASIAN GRILLED CHICKEN WITH BOK CHOY

Preparation time: 10 minutes + marinating
Total cooking time: 15–20 minutes
Serves 4

4 tablespoons honey
3 tablespoons oil
1 tablespoon grated fresh ginger
2 teaspoons sweet chilli sauce
1½ teaspoons Chinese five-spice powder
8 chicken thighs
500 g (1 1b 2 oz) bok choy (pak choy)
250 ml (9 fl oz/1 cup) chicken stock

1 Combine honey, oil, ginger, chilli sauce and five-spice in a small bowl. Place chicken thighs in a large non-metal dish. Pour honey mixture over chicken thighs. Cover and refrigerate for several hours or overnight. Drain chicken and reserve marinade.
2 Place chicken on cold, lightly oiled grill (broiler) tray; brush with reserved marinade. Cook under medium–high heat for 15–20 minutes or until tender, brushing with honey mixture several times during cooking. Turn chicken occasionally.
3 Meanwhile, rinse bok choy, pat dry and trim off excess stems. Place chicken stock in a medium pan and bring to the boil. Add bok choy; cover pan. Reduce heat to low and simmer for 3 minutes or until tender. Drain bok choy and arrange on serving plates. Place cooked chicken on top.

COOK'S FILE

Storage time: Cook chicken just before serving.
Note: Bok choy is a green leafy vegetable, similar to spinach. It is available from most fruit and vegetable stores. However, if unavailable, English spinach or silverbeet (Swiss chard) may be used instead.

1

2

3

GRILLED CHICKEN BREAST WITH BARBECUE GLAZE

Preparation time: 10 minutes
+ marinating
Total cooking time: 10 minutes
Serves 4

4 tablespoons barbecue sauce
1 tablespoon honey
3 tablespoons mayonnaise
2 garlic cloves, crushed
2 teaspoons grated fresh ginger
4 skinless, boneless chicken breasts

1 Combine barbecue sauce, honey, mayonnaise, garlic and ginger in a medium bowl. Add chicken fillets to bowl, toss until well coated. Cover and reingerate for several hours or overnight.

2 Place chicken on cold, lightly oiled grill (broiler) tray. Cook, brushing occasionally with remaining marinade, under high heat 5–8 minutes. Turn and cook other side for 5–8 minutes or until chicken is tender. Slice chicken for serving. Serve with a green salad.

COOK'S FILE

Variations: The glaze in this recipe is suitable for other cuts of chicken such as thigh fillets and wings.

1

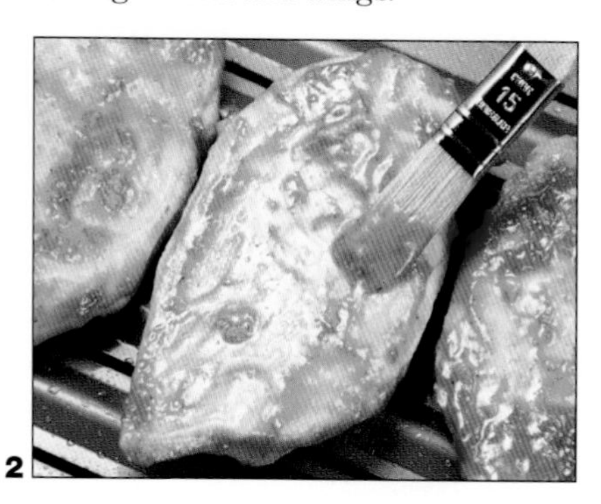

2

Pan-fries and stir-fries

SAUSAGES AND MASH WITH FRENCH SHALLOT GRAVY

Preparation time: 15 minutes
Cooking time: 25 minutes
Serves 4

4 tablespoons olive oil
200 g (7 oz) French shallots, peeled and thinly sliced
1 tablespoon plain (all-purpose) flour
125 ml (4 fl oz/½ cup) red wine
375 ml (13 fl oz/1½ cups) good-quality beef stock
1 tablespoon dijon mustard
1.5 kg (3 lb 5 oz) potatoes, chopped
150 g (5½ oz) butter
8 thick good-quality pork sausages (about 100 g/ 3½ oz each)
450 g (1 lb) green beans, top and tailed

1 Heat 2 tablespoons of the oil in a large frying pan over medium heat. Add the French shallots and cook for 5 minutes, stirring often until they soften and become transparent. Add the flour and cook for 30 seconds. Increase the heat to high, pour in the wine and stock and bring to the boil. Reduce the heat to medium and simmer for 10 minutes, or until the gravy thickens and reduces. Stir in the mustard, then reduce the heat to medium–low and simmer gently until the sausages and mash are ready.

2 Meanwhile, cook the potatoes in a large saucepan of boiling water for 12–15 minutes, or until tender. Drain and return to the pan with 1 tablespoon of olive oil and 120 g (4¼ oz) of the butter. Mash with a potato masher until smooth and creamy, then season to taste with salt and freshly ground black pepper.

3 While the potatoes are cooking, prick the sausages with a fork. Heat a large frying pan over medium–high heat, add a tablespoon of oil and add the sausages. Cook for 10 minutes, or until cooked through, turning often to brown evenly.

4 Bring a saucepan of lightly salted water to the boil, then add the beans and cook for 4 minutes, or until just tender. Whisk the remaining butter into the gravy and season. To serve, place a mound of mash on each plate, top with the sausages and gravy, and serve with the beans on the side.

COOK'S FILE

Note: To save time, slice 200 g (7 oz) red onions instead of the French shallots.

1

VEAL SCALOPPINE WITH SAGE

Preparation time: 15 minutes
Cooking time: 1 hour
Serves 4

600 g (1 lb 5 oz) small new potatoes, halved
4 tablespoons olive oil
8 small (600 g/1 lb 5 oz) veal scaloppine fillets or schnitzels
4 slices pancetta, cut in half lengthways
8 fresh sage leaves
250 ml (9 fl oz/1 cup) marsala
250 g (9 oz) asparagus spears

1 Preheat the oven to 200°C (400°F/Gas 6). Cook the potatoes in a large saucepan of boiling water for 10 minutes. Drain and transfer to a baking tray with 2 tablespoons of the olive oil. Toss well and bake for 40–50 minutes, or until crisp.

2 Meanwhile, pound each veal fillet between two sheets of plastic wrap with a mallet or rolling pin until, 5 mm (¼ inch) thick. Press a piece of pancetta and a sage leaf onto each scaloppine fillet, then skewer with a toothpick. Season well with salt and freshly ground black pepper.

3 Heat remaining oil in a large heavy-based frying pan. Place the scaloppine pancetta-side-down in the pan and cook for 1–2 minutes. Turn and cook for another minute. Remove from the pan and keep warm (you may have to do this in two batches). Add the marsala and cook for 4–5 minutes, or until syrupy and reduced by half. Return the scaloppine to the pan and toss lightly in the sauce until warmed through.

4 When the potatoes are nearly ready, bring a large saucepan of salted water to the boil. Add the asparagus and cook for 3 minutes. Drain.

5 To serve, remove the toothpicks from the scaloppine and divide among four serving plates. Drizzle any pan juices on top. Serve with the asparagus and roast potatoes on the side.

1

FILLET STEAK WITH MIXED MUSHROOMS AND SHERRY

Preparation time: 10 minutes
Cooking time: 20 minutes
Serves 4

250 g (9 oz) broccoli, cut into large florets
250 g (9 oz) green beans, top and tailed
1 tablespoon oil
60 g (2¼ oz) butter
4 rib eye steaks (scotch fillet) (about 160 g/5½ oz each), 2.5 cm (1 inch) thick
3 garlic cloves, finely chopped
250 g (9 oz) mixed mushrooms (portabella, Swiss brown shiitake or button)
2 teaspoons chopped fresh thyme
125 ml (4 fl oz/½ cup) dry sherry

1 Bring a saucepan of lightly salted water to the boil. Add the broccoli and beans and cook for 3–4 minutes, or until tender but still crisp. Drain.
2 Melt the oil and 1 tablespoons of the butter in a large stainless steel frying pan. Cook the steaks for 3–4 minutes on each side for medium–rare, or until cooked to your liking. Remove from the pan, cover with foil and rest.
3 Melt another tablespoon of butter in the pan over medium heat. Add the garlic and mushrooms and season to taste. Cook for 3–4 minutes, or until the mushrooms have softened. Stir in the thyme. Remove from the pan.
4 Add the sherry and any juices from the rested meat to the pan and stir well to scrape up any sediment stuck to the base. Bring to the boil, then reduce the heat and simmer for 2–3 minutes, or until reduced to 4 tablespoons and thickened slightly. Whisk in the remaining butter in small amounts, until glossy.
5 To serve, put the steaks on four serving plates, top with the mushrooms and spoon the sauce over the top. Serve with the broccoli and green beans.

COOK'S FILE

Note: Exotic mushrooms are available pre-packaged in most supermarkets.

1

2

SWORDFISH WITH TOMATO SALSA AND GARLIC MASH

Preparation time: 15 minutes
Cooking time: 25 minutes
Serves 4

500 g (1 lb 2 oz) potatoes, cubed
2 large vine-ripened tomatoes
2 tablespoons finely shredded fresh basil
1 tablespoon balsamic vinegar
3 garlic cloves, finely chopped
145 ml (4¾ fl oz) olive oil
4 swordfish steaks (about 200 g/7 oz each)

1 Cook the potato in a large saucepan of boiling water for 12–15 minutes, or until tender.

2 To make the salsa, score a cross in the base of each tomato. Place in a heatproof bowl and cover with boiling water. Leave for 30 seconds, then plunge into iced water and peel the skin away from the cross. Cut the tomatoes in half, scoop out the seeds with a teaspoon and discard. Finely dice the flesh, then combine with the basil, vinegar, 2 cloves of the garlic and 2 tablespoons of the oil. Season.

Heat 3 tablespoons of the olive oil in a large non-stick frying pan over medium–high heat. Season the swordfish well, then add to the frying pan and cook for 2–3 minutes on each side for medium–rare, or until cooked to your liking.

3 Just before the swordfish is ready, drain the potatoes. Add the remaining olive oil and garlic, and season to taste. Mash until smooth.

4 To serve, put the swordfish steaks on four serving plates and top with the tomato salsa. Serve the garlic mash on the side.

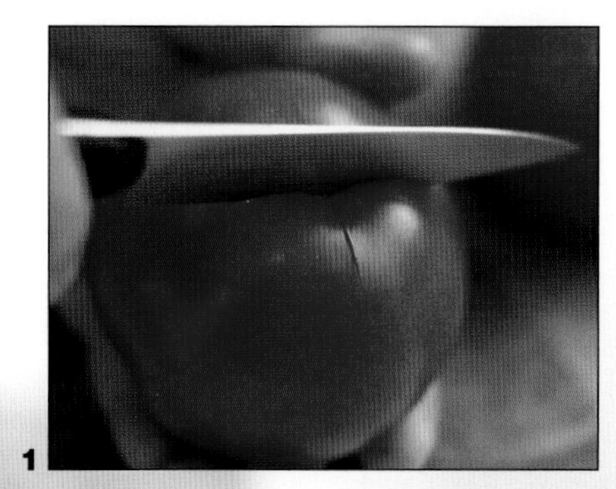
1

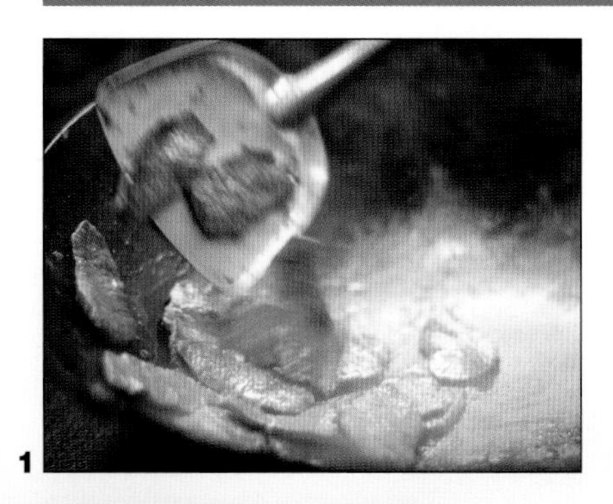
1

LAMB, MINT AND CHILLI STIR-FRY

Preparation time: 10 minutes
Cooking time: 15 minutes
Serves 4

250 g (9 oz/1¼ cups) jasmine rice
2 tablespoons oil
750 g (1 lb 10 oz) lamb backstrap, thinly sliced
2 garlic cloves, finely chopped
1 small red onion, cut into wedges
1 fresh bird's eye chilli, finely chopped
3 tablespoons lime juice
2 tablespoons sweet chilli sauce
2 tablespoons fish sauce
10 g (¼ oz/½ cup) fresh mint leaves

1 Bring a large saucepan of water to the boil. Add the rice and cook for 12 minutes, stirring occasionally. Drain well.

2 Meanwhile, heat a wok until very hot, add 1 tablespoon oil and swirl to coat. Add the lamb in batches and cook for 2 minutes, or until browned. Remove from the wok.

3 Heat the remaining oil in the wok, add the garlic and onion and stir-fry for 1 minute, then add the chilli and cook for 30 seconds. Return the lamb to the wok, then add the lime juice, sweet chilli sauce and fish sauce and stir-fry for 2 minutes over high heat. Stir in the mint and serve with the rice.

COOK'S FILE

Variation: Try chicken breasts or pork loin, adding 80 g (2¾ oz/½ cup) cashews and basil instead of mint.

SALT AND PEPPER CHICKEN WITH ASIAN GREENS AND OYSTER SAUCE

Preparation time: 15 minutes
Cooking time: 20 minutes
Serves 4

250 g (9 oz/1¼ cups) jasmine rice
4 tablespoons plain (all-purpose) flour
¾ teaspoon five-spice powder
1½ teaspoons fine sea salt
1 teaspoon ground white pepper
750 g (1 lb 10 oz) skinless, boneless chicken breasts, cut into thin strips
145 ml (4¾ fl oz) peanut oil
1.25 kg (2 lb 12 oz) mixed Asian greens
125 ml (4 fl oz/½ cup) oyster sauce

1 Preheat the oven to 200°C (400°F/Gas 6). Bring a large saucepan of water to the boil. Add the rice and cook for 12 minutes, stirring occasionally. Drain well.

2 Meanwhile, combine the flour, five-spice powder, salt and pepper in a large bowl. Toss the chicken strips in the flour until well coated. Heat 3 tablespoons of the oil in a large frying pan over medium–high heat. Add the chicken in three batches and cook, turning, for about 3 minutes, or until browned. Drain on crumpled paper towels and keep warm.

3 Heat the remaining oil and cook the mixed Asian greens over medium–high heat for 1–2 minutes. Add the oyster sauce and toss through. Serve on a bed of jasmine rice topped with the chicken strips.

1

2

LAMB FILLETS WITH BEAN AND ROSEMARY PURÉE

Preparation time: 10 minutes
Total cooking time: 5–10 minutes
Serves 4

1 tablespoon oil
4 small lamb fillets

Bean and rosemary purée
400 g (14 oz) tin cannellini beans, drained
4 tablespoons olive oil
3 teaspoons chopped rosemary
2 teaspoons lemon juice
½ teaspoon ground paprika
2 garlic cloves, crushed
salt and pepper, to season

1 Heat oil in large frying pan; add lamb fillets. Sear over high heat 2–3 minutes each side. For rare meat, cook another minute each side. For medium and well-done fillets, reduce heat to medium. Continue cooking another 2–3 minutes each side for medium fillets and 4–6 minutes each side for well-done. Remove from pan; drain on paper towels. Cover, keep warm for 5 minutes. Cut lamb fillets into thin diagonal slices. Serve with bean and rosemary purée.

2 To make bean and rosemary purée, combine beans, oil, rosemary, lemon juice, paprika, garlic, salt and pepper in food processor or blender. Blend 30 seconds or until smooth. Transfer purée to small pan; stir over medium heat 1 minute or until heated through. May be served with pan-fried onion slices and steamed vegetables.

CHICKEN SAN CHOY BAU

Preparation time: 10 minutes
Total cooking time: 5 minutes
Serves 4

1 tablespoon oil
700 g (1 lb 9 oz) minced (ground) chicken
2 garlic cloves, finely chopped
100 g (3½ oz) tin water chestnuts, drained, chopped
1½ tablespoons oyster sauce
3 teaspoons soy sauce
1 teaspoon sugar
5 spring onions (scallions), finely sliced
4 whole lettuce leaves

1 Heat a wok or frying pan over high heat; add the oil and swirl to coat. Add the chicken mince and garlic and stir-fry for 3–4 minutes, or until browned and cooked through, breaking up any lumps with the back of a spoon. Pour off any excess liquid.
2 Reduce the heat and add the water chestnuts, oyster sauce, soy sauce, sugar and spring onion.
3 Trim the lettuce leaves around the edges to neaten them and to form a cup shape. Divide the chicken and vegetable mixture among the lettuce cups and serve hot, with extra oyster sauce, if desired.

1

2

3

PORK CHOPS WITH APPLE AND RED ONION CHUTNEY

Preparation time: 15 minutes
Cooking time: 30 minutes
Serves 4

125 g (4½ oz) butter
2 small red onions, sliced
2 Granny Smith apples, peeled, cored, then cut into quarters and sliced
¼ teaspoon ground cloves
4 tablespoons honey
4 pork loin chops (about 250 g/9 oz each)
2 teaspoons oil
½ teaspoon caraway seeds
725 g (1 lb 9 oz) green cabbage, thinly shredded

1 To make the chutney, melt 50 g (1¾ oz) of the butter in a saucepan, then add the onion, apple, cloves and honey. Simmer, covered, for 10 minutes over low heat. Increase the heat to medium and cook, uncovered, for a further 20 minutes, or until the liquid is reduced to a thick chutney. Allow to cool.

2 Meanwhile, season the chops well on both sides with salt and freshly ground black pepper. Heat the oil and 50 g (1¾ oz) of the butter in a large frying pan and sauté the chops over medium–high heat for 6–8 minutes on each side, or until browned and cooked through. Remove the pan from the heat, leaving the chops to rest for 2 minutes.

3 Melt remaining butter in a large saucepan, add the caraway seeds and green cabbage, and cook, covered, over medium–low heat, tossing a few times with tongs, for 12 minutes, or until tender.

4 To serve, place a pork chop on each serving plate and serve the cabbage on the side. Dollop with a spoonful of chutney.

COOK'S FILE

Note: Resting the chops for a couple of minutes before serving allows the juices to settle evenly throughout the chop, resulting in lovely moist meat.

VEAL SCHNITZEL WITH DILL POTATO SALAD

Preparation time: 15 minutes
Cooking time: 25 minutes
Serves 4

750 g (1 lb 10 oz) desiree potatoes, unpeeled
500 g (1 lb 2 oz) veal leg steaks
60 g (2¼ oz/½ cup) seasoned plain (all-purpose) flour
2 eggs, lightly beaten
100 g (3½ oz/1 cup) dry breadcrumbs
125 ml (4 fl oz/½ cup) virgin olive oil
2 tablespoons lemon juice
1½ tablespoons finely chopped fresh dill
200 g (7 oz) mixed salad leaves

1 Cook the potatoes in a large saucepan of boiling water for 15–20 minutes, or until tender. Drain. Cut into quarters lengthways and cover to keep warm.
2 Meanwhile, beat the veal between two sheets of plastic wrap to 5 mm (¼ inch) thickness. Coat the veal in the flour and shake off the excess. Dip the veal in the egg, then coat in breadcrumbs. Place the schnitzel on a flat tray, cover and freeze for 5 minutes.
3 Heat 3 tablespoons of oil in a large frying pan and cook the veal in two batches, over medium–high heat for 2–3 minutes on each side, or until golden and cooked through. Drain on crumpled paper towel and keep warm.
4 Whisk the lemon juice, dill and remaining oil together in a small bowl and pour over the potatoes. Season with salt and freshly ground black pepper and toss gently. Serve the schnitzel with the potatoes and a mixed salad.

COOK'S FILE

Hint: Snip the edges of the veal with scissors to prevent the sides curling during cooking.

1

TERIYAKI CHICKEN WITH GINGER CHIVE RICE

Preparation time: 10 minutes + 1 hour marinating
Cooking time: 20 minutes
Serves 4

4 small skinless, boneless chicken breasts, skin on (about 170 g/6 oz each)
3 tablespoons Japanese soy sauce
2 tablespoons sake
1½ tablespoons mirin
1½ tablespoons soft brown sugar
3 teaspoons finely grated fresh ginger
300 g (10½ oz/1½ cups) long-grain rice
2 tablespoons finely chopped fresh chives
2 tablespoons oil

1 Pound each breast between two sheets of plastic wrap with a mallet or rolling pin until 1 cm (½ inch) thick.

2 Place the soy sauce, sake, mirin, sugar and 1 teaspoon of the ginger in a flat non-metallic dish big enough to fit all the chicken in a single layer and stir until the sugar has dissolved. Add the chicken and turn to emit. Cover and refrigerate for 1 hour, turning once halfway through.

3 Once the chicken has marinated, bring a large saucepan of water to the boil. Add the rice and cook for 12 minutes, stirring occasionally. Drain. Stir in the chives and the remaining ginger, then cover until ready to serve.

4 Meanwhile, drain the chicken, reserving the marinade. Heat the oil in a large deep frying pan and cook the chicken, skin-side-down over medium heat for 4–5 minutes, or until the skin is crisp. Turn and cook the other side for 4 minutes—remove from the pan (the chicken should not be quite cooked through).

5 Add the reserved marinade and 3 tablespoons water to the pan and scrape any sediment stuck to the base. Bring to the boil over high heat, then return the chicken (skin-side-up) with any juices to the pan. Cook for 5–6 minutes, or until just cooked through, turning once to coat. (If the sauce is still a little runny, remove the chicken and boil the sauce over high heat until it is slightly syrupy.) Rest the chicken for a few minutes.

6 To serve, divide the rice among four serving plates and place the chicken (either whole or sliced on the diagonal) on top. Drizzle with a little sauce and serve with steamed Asian greens.

CARAMEL PORK AND PUMPKIN STIR-FRY

Preparation time: 15 minutes
Cooking time: 20 minutes
Serves 4

250 g (9 oz/1¼ cups) jasmine rice
300 g (10½ oz) butternut pumpkin
500 g (1 lb 2 oz) pork fillet
2 garlic cloves, crushed
2–3 tablespoons peanut oil
4 tablespoons soft brown sugar
3 tablespoons fish sauce
3 tablespoons rice vinegar
2 tablespoons chopped fresh coriander (cilantro) leaves
1.25 kg (2 lb 12 oz) mixed Asian greens

1 Bring a large saucepan of water to the boil. Add the rice and cook for 12 minutes, stirring occasionally. Drain well.
2 Meanwhile, cut the pumpkin into pieces roughly 2 cm x 4 cm (¾ inch x 1¼ inch) and 5 mm (¼ inch) thick. Thinly slice the pork, then combine with the garlic and 2 teaspoons of the peanut oil. Season with salt and plenty of pepper.
3 Heat a wok until very hot, add 1 tablespoon oil and swirl to coat. When just starting to smoke, stir-fry the pork in two batches for about 1 minute per batch, or until the meat changes colour. Transfer to a plate. Add the remaining oil to the wok and stir-fry the pumpkin for 4 minutes, or until tender but not falling apart. Remove and add to the pork.
4 Combine the sugar, fish sauce, rice vinegar and 125 ml (4 fl oz/½ cup) water in the wok and boil for about 10 minutes, or until syrupy. Return the pork and pumpkin to the wok and stir for 1 minute, or until well coated and heated through. Stir in the coriander.
5 Place the mixed Asian greens, in a paper-lined bamboo steamer over a wok of simmering water for 3 minutes, or until wilted. Serve immediately with the stir-fry and rice.

1

2

CRUMBED CALAMARI WITH CHILLI PLUM SAUCE

Preparation time: 25 minutes
Total cooking time: 12 minutes
Serves 4

500 g (1 lb 2 oz) calamari tubes
3 tablespoons plain (all-purpose) flour
1–2 eggs, lightly beaten
240 g (8½ oz/3 cups) fresh breadcrumbs
oil, for frying

Chilli plum sauce
1 teaspoon oil
1 garlic clove, crushed
315 g (11oz/1 cup) dark plum jam
4 tablespoons white vinegar
1–2 tablespoons bottled chopped chilli or sweet chilli sauce

1 Rinse calamari tubes and pat dry with paper towels. Remove spine and skin if necessary. Cut into 1 cm (½ inch) rings. Set aside.
2 Combine flour, salt and pepper in a plastic bag. Add calamari and toss to coat. Dip each ring into beaten egg, drain off excess; toss in breadcrumbs. Pat crumbs lightly onto rings, shake off excess. Heat 2 cm (¾ inch) of oil in a frying pan until hot.
3 Fry a few calamari rings at a time, until golden. Drain on paper towels. Keep warm. Use slotted spoon to remove crumbs from surface of oil between batches. Serve rings hot, with a bowl of chilli plum sauce. If desired, serve with wedges of lemon.
4 To make chilli plum sauce, heat oil in a small pan. Add garlic and cook until just starting to colour. Add jam, vinegar and chilli. Stir over medium heat until well blended. Thin with a little warm water if necessary.

1

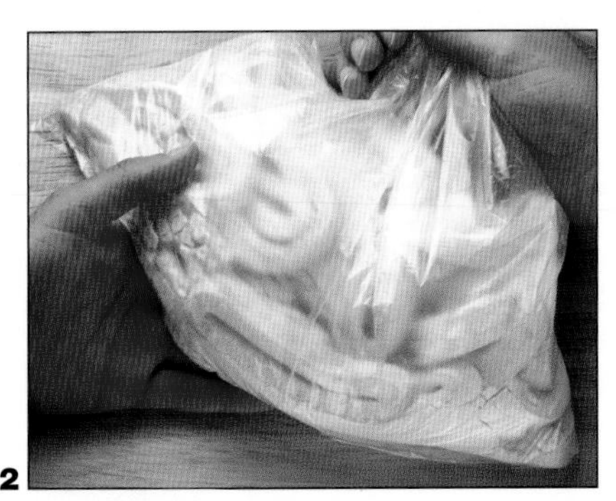

2

3

ASIAN RISSOLES

Preparation time: 15 minutes
Total cooking time: 30 minutes
Serves 4

600 g (1 lb 5 oz) minced (ground) chicken
2 tablespoons sweet chilli sauce
2 tablespoons coriander (cilantro), roughly chopped
2 stalks lemongrass, white part only, finely chopped
2 egg whites, lightly beaten
110 g (3¾ oz/1⅓ cups) fresh breadcrumbs
100 g (3½ oz/⅔ cup) sesame seeds
2–3 tablespoons oil

1 Preheat the oven to 200°C (400°F/Gas 6). Combine minced chicken, sweet chilli sauce, coriander, lemongrass, egg white and breadcrumbs. Season well with salt and pepper. Divide the mixture into 8 portions and shape into rissoles. Coat with the sesame seeds.
2 Heat the oil in a frying pan and cook the rissoles, in batches, for 3–4 minutes each side, or until the crust is golden.
3 Place the rissoles on a lined oven tray and bake for 15 minutes, or until cooked through. Serve the rissoles with a green salad and potato wedges or as a burger.

1

2

3

1

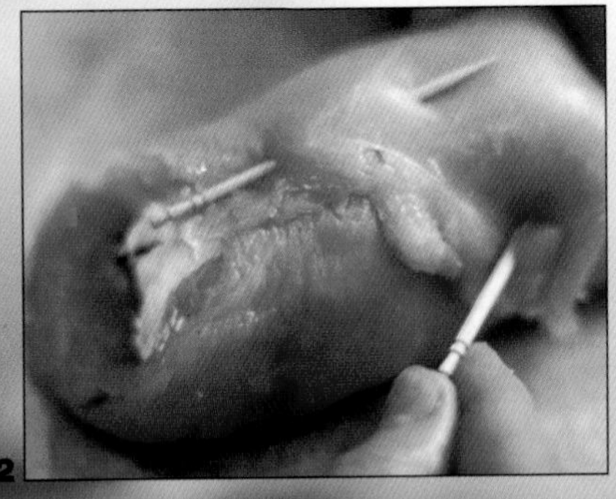
2

STUFFED CHICKEN BREAST WITH TOMATO, GOAT'S CHEESE AND ASPARAGUS

Preparation time: 15 minutes
Cooking time: 20 minutes
Serves 4

4 large skinless, boneless chicken breasts
100 g (3½ oz) semi-dried (sun-blushed) tomatoes
100 g (3½ oz) mild goat's cheese, sliced
200 g (7 oz) asparagus spears, trimmed, halved and blanched
50 g (1¾ oz) butter
375 ml (13 fl oz/1½ cups) chicken stock
2 zucchini (courgettes), cut into 5 cm (2 inch) batons
250 ml (9 fl oz/1 cup) cream
8 spring onions (scallions), thinly sliced

1 Pound each chicken breast between two sheets of plastic wrap with a mallet or rolling pin until 1 cm (½ inch) thick. Divide the tomato, goat's cheese 155 g (5½ oz) of the asparagus pieces among the breasts. Roll up tightly lengthways, securing along the seam with toothpicks.

2 Heat the butter in a large frying pan over medium heat. Add the chicken and brown on all sides. Pour in stock, then reduce the heat, to low. Cook, covered, for 10 minutes, or until the chicken is cooked through. Remove the chicken and keep warm.

3 Meanwhile, bring a saucepan of lightly salted water to the boil. Add the zucchini and remaining asparagus and cook for 2 minutes or until just tender. Remove from the pan. Whisk the cream into the frying pan. Add the spring onion and simmer over medium–low heat for 4 minutes, or until reduced and thickened.

4 To serve, cut each chicken roll in half on the diagonal and place on serving plates. Spoon on the sauce and serve with the greens.

1

2

LAMB CUTLETS WITH TANGY GARLIC AND THYME SAUCE

Preparation time: 10 minutes
Total cooking time: 10 minutes
Serves 2

2 tablespoons oil
4 lamb cutlets
3 tablespoons white wine
4 tablespoons thick (double/ heavy) cream
4 garlic cloves, crushed
1 tablespoon chopped thyme

1 Place oil in large frying pan. Trim excess fat and sinew from lamb cutlets. Heat oil, add chops to pan. Cook over high heat 3 minutes each side or until brown, turning once. Remove from pan; drain off excess fat.

2 Add wine, cream, garlic and chopped thyme to pan; bring to the boil. Reduce heat to low, simmer for 2 minutes or until liquid is reduced by half. Return drained chops to pan, simmer for 2 minutes or until chops are tender. Garnish with thyme, if desired.

COOK'S FILE

Variation: Use lamb loin or chump chops. Trim off any excess fat.

1

FISH WITH MARJORAM AND LIME

Preparation time: 15 minutes
Total cooking time: 4 minutes
Serves 4

100 g (3½ oz/1 cup) dried breadcrumbs
2 teaspoons dried marjoram
1 teaspoon cayenne pepper
4 ling fillets
1 egg, lightly beaten
3 tablespoons oil
2 tablespoons lime juice

1 Combine breadcrumbs, marjoram and cayenne pepper on a sheet of greaseproof paper.
2 Brush fish fillets with egg, coat with breadcrumb mixture. Heat oil in pan; add fish. Cook over medium heat for 2 minutes each side or until tender and golden brown. Serve drizzled with lime juice. Garnish with fresh marjoram, if desired.

COOK'S FILE

Storage time: Fish can be coated in breadcrumb mixture several hours ahead. Store, covered, in refrigerator. Cook just before serving.
Variation: Any white, firm-fleshed fish fillets are suitable for this recipe.

CRUNCHY FISH FILLETS

Preparation time: 10 minutes
Total cooking time: 6 minutes
Serves 4

150 g (5½ oz/½ cup) polenta (cornmeal)
4 bream fillets
3 tablespoons oil
170 g (6 oz/⅔ cup) mayonnaise
2 tablespoons chopped chives
1 tablespoon sweet chilli sauce

1 Place cornmeal on a sheet of greaseproof paper or plate.
2 Cut diagonal slashes in skin of fish fillets. Press fillets in cornmeal to coat thoroughly. Heat oil in pan; add the coated fish.
3 Cook over medium heat for 3 minutes on each side, or until tender. Drain on paper towels. Combine mayonnaise, chives and chilli sauce. Serve with fish. Garnish with chervil, if desired.

COOK'S FILE

Variation: Any firm-fleshed fish is suitable for this recipe

1

2

TOFU, SNOW PEA AND MUSHROOM STIR-FRY

Preparation time: 10 minutes
Cooking time: 15 minutes
Serves 4

250 g (9 oz/1¼ cups) jasmine rice
3 tablespoons peanut oil
600 g (1 lb 5 oz) firm tofu, drained, cut into 2 cm (¾ inch) cubes
2 teaspoons sambal oelek or chilli paste
2 garlic cloves, finely chopped
400 g (14 oz) fresh Asian mushrooms, sliced (shiitake, oyster or black fungus)
300 g (10½ oz) snow peas (mangetout), trimmed
3 tablespoons kecap manis

1 Bring a large saucepan of water to the boil. Add the rice and cook for 12 minutes, stirring occasionally. Drain well.

2 Meanwhile, heat a wok until very hot. Add 2 tablespoons of the oil and swirl to coat. Stir-fry the tofu in two batches on all sides for 2–3 minutes, or until lightly browned, then transfer to a plate.

3 Add the remaining oil to the wok, add the sambal oelek, garlic, mushrooms, snow peas and 1 tablespoon water and stir-fry for 1–2 minutes, or until the vegetables are almost cooked but still crunchy.

4 Return tofu to the wok, add kecap manis and stir-fry for another minute, or until heated through and combined. Serve immediately with rice.

COOK'S FILE

Note: Firm tofu is suitable to stir-fry as it will hold its shape.

Variation: Use 3 teaspoons grated fresh ginger instead of the sambal oelek.

1

2

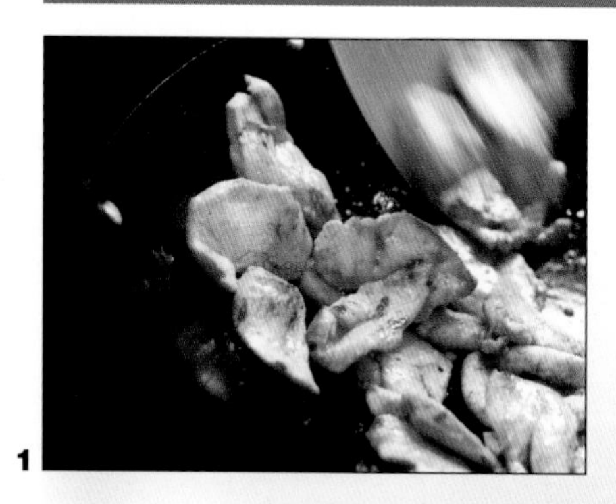
1

SATAY CHICKEN STIR-FRY

Preparation time: 10 minutes
Cooking time: 20 minutes
Serves 4

250 g (9 oz/1½ cups) jasmine rice
1½ tablespoons peanut oil
6 spring onions (scallions), cut into 3 cm (1¼ inch) lengths
800 g (1 lb 2 oz) skinless, boneless chicken breasts, thinly sliced on the diagonal
1–1½ tablespoons good-quality Thai red curry paste
4 tablespoons crunchy peanut butter
270 ml (9½ fl oz) coconut milk
2 teaspoons soft brown sugar
1½ tablespoons lime juice

1 Bring a large saucepan of water to the boil. Add the rice and cook for 12 minutes, stirring occasionally. Drain well.

2 Meanwhile, heat a wok until very hot, add 1 teaspoon of the peanut oil and swirl to coat. When hot, add the spring onion and stir-fry for 30 seconds, or until softened slightly. Remove from the wok. Add a little extra peanut oil to the wok as needed and stir-fry the chicken in three batches for about 1 minute per batch, or until the meat just changes colour. Remove from the wok.

3 Add a little more oil to the wok, add the curry paste and stir-fry for 1 minute, or until fragrant. Add the peanut butter, coconut milk, sugar and 250 ml (9 fl oz/1 cup) water and stir well. Bring to the boil and boil for 3–4 minutes, or until thickened and the oil starts to separate—reduce the heat slightly if the sauce spits at you. Return the chicken and the spring onion to the wok, stir well and cook for 2 minutes, or until heated through. Stir in the lime juice and season. Serve at once with the rice and a crisp green salad.

BEAN ENCHILADAS

Preparation time: 20 minutes
Total cooking time: 25 minutes
Serves 4

1 tablespoon light olive oil
1 onion, finely sliced
3 garlic cloves, crushed
1 bird's eye chilli, finely chopped
2 teaspoons ground cumin
125 ml (4 fl oz/½ cup) vegetable stock
3 tomatoes, peeled, deseeded and chopped
1 tablespoon tomato paste (concentrated purée)
2 x 430 g (15 oz) tins three-bean mix
2 tablespoons chopped coriander (cilantro) leaves
8 flour tortillas
1 small avocado, peeled and chopped
125 g (4½ oz/½ cup) light sour cream
4 tablespoons coriander (cilantro) sprigs
115 g (4 oz/2 cups) shredded lettuce

1 Heat the oil in a deep frying pan over medium heat. Add the onion and cook for 3–4 minutes, or until just soft. Add the garlic and chilli and cook for a further 30 seconds. Add the cumin, vegetable stock, tomatoes and tomato paste and cook for 6–8 minutes, or until the mixture is quite thick and pulpy. Season with salt and freshly ground black pepper.
2 Preheat the oven to 170°C (325°F/Gas 3). Drain and rinse the beans. Add the beans to the sauce and cook for 5 minutes to heat through, then add the chopped coriander.
3 Meanwhile, wrap the tortillas in foil and warm in the oven for 3–4 minutes.
4 Place a tortilla on a plate and spread with 3 tablespoons of the bean mixture. Top with some avocado, sour cream, coriander sprigs and lettuce. Roll the enchiladas up, tucking in the ends. Cut each one in half to serve.

Cook the tomato sauce until the mixture is thick and pulpy.

Place the filling in the centre of the tortilla and roll up, tucking in the ends.

CHICKEN STIR-FRY WITH SNOWPEA SPROUTS

Preparation time: 15 minutes
Total cooking time: 15 minutes
Serves 4

2 tablespoons oil
1 onion, finely sliced
3 makrut (kaffir lime) leaves, shredded
3 skinless, boneless chicken breasts, cut into 2 cm (¾ inch) cubes
1 red capsicum (pepper), sliced
3 tablespoons lime juice
100 ml (3½ fl oz) soy sauce
100 g (3½ oz) snowpea (mangetout) sprouts
2 tablespoons chopped coriander (cilantro) leaves

1 Heat a wok or frying pan over medium heat, add the oil and swirl to coat. Add the onion and makrut leaves and stir-fry for 3–5 minutes, or until the onion begins to soften. Add the chicken and cook for a further 4 minutes. Add the capsicum and continue to cook for 2–3 minutes.

2 Stir in the lime juice and soy sauce and cook for 1–2 minutes, or until the sauce reduces slightly. Add the sprouts and coriander. Cook until the sprouts have wilted. Serve with steamed rice, and coriander and chilli, if desired.

1

2

COOK'S FILE

Variation: Use chicken, soy sauce and lime juice as a base, and add or subtract ingredients to your taste.

PAN-FRIED LAMB FILLETS WITH RED WINE

Preparation time: 10 minutes
Cooking time: 20 minutes
Serves 4

600 g (1 lb 5 oz) small new potatoes
160 g (5½ oz) snow peas (mangetout), trimmed
2 tablespoons olive oil
4 lamb backstraps or eye of loin fillets (about 200 g/ 7 oz each), trimmed
170 ml (5½ fl oz/⅔ cup) red wine
1 tablespoon redcurrant jelly
2 teaspoons chopped fresh thyme
30 g (1 oz) butter, chilled and cut into cubes

1 Cook the potatoes in a large saucepan of lightly salted boiling water for 15–20 minutes, or until tender. Add the snow peas and cook for a further 1 minute. Drain the vegetables, return to the pan and toss gently with 1 tablespoon of the oil.
2 Meanwhile, heat the remaining oil in a large frying pan and cook the lamb fillets over medium–high heat for 4–5 minutes, or until cooked, but still pink inside. Remove from the pan, cover and keep warm.
3 Add the wine, redcurrant jelly and thyme to the pan and bring to the boil. Boil rapidly for 5 minutes, or until reduced and syrupy. Stir in the butter.
4 To serve, slice the lamb on the diagonal, divide among four plates and spoon some of the sauce on top. Serve with the vegetables.

1

BEER-BATTERED FISH FILLETS WITH CHIPS

Preparation time: 15 minutes
Cooking time: 15 minutes
Serves 4

3 tablespoons self-raising flour
3 tablespoons cornflour (cornstarch)
125 g (4½ oz/1 cup) plain (all-purpose) flour
250 ml (9 fl oz/1 cup) beer
oil, for deep-frying
4 large pontiac potatoes, cut into finger-size chips

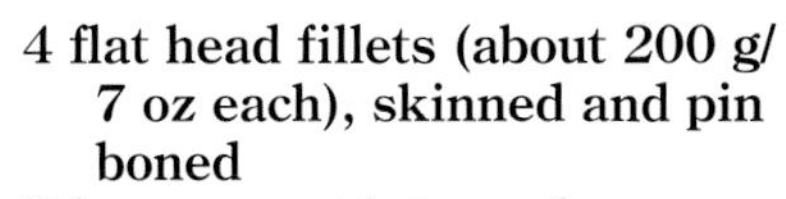

4 flat head fillets (about 200 g/ 7 oz each), skinned and pin boned
2 lemons, cut into wedges

1 Preheat oven to 180°C (350°F/ Gas 4). Sift self-raising flour, cornflour and 60 g (2¼ oz/½ cup) of the plain flour in to a large bowl and make a well in the centre. Gradually whisk in beer to make a smooth batter. Cover.
2 Fill a large heavy-based saucepan one-third full of oil and heat to 180°C (350°F), or until a cube of bread dropped into the oil browns in 15 seconds. Deep-fry the potato chips in batches for 2–4 minutes, or until pale golden. Drain on paper towels. Deep-fry again for 3 minutes, or until golden and cooked through. Keep hot in the oven while you cook the fish.
3 Reheat the oil to 180°C (350°F). Stir batter, then coat the fish fillets in the remaining plain flour, shaking off the excess. Dip the fillets into the batter, allowing the excess to drip off a little. Slowly ease the fillets into the hot oil, holding the tail out for a few seconds—turn with tongs if necessary. Cook for 4–5 minutes, or until golden and the fish is cooked through. Remove with a slotted spoon and drain on crumpled paper towel. Serve with chips, lemon wedges and a green salad.

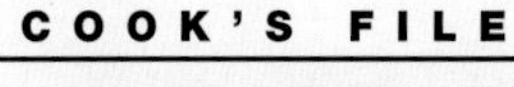

COOK'S FILE

Hint: Use any type of white fish fillets (for example snapper, blue eye cod or John Dory) and any type of beer to vary the flavour.

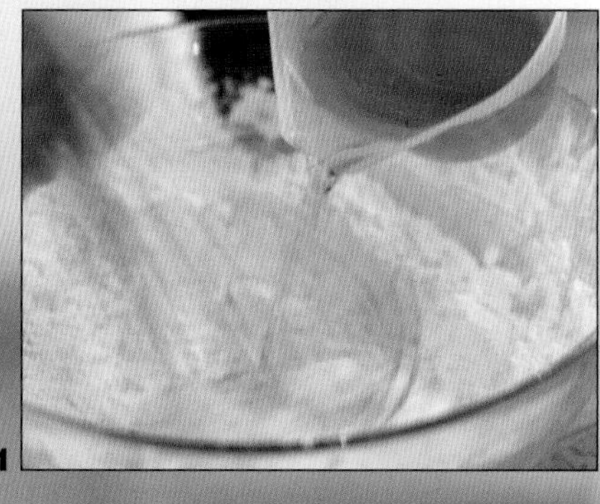
1

2

TUNA STEAKS WITH OLIVE MAYONNAISE AND POTATO WEDGES

Preparation time: 15 minutes
Cooking time: 50 minutes
Serves 4

3 large pontiac potatoes, unpeeled and cut lengthways into 8 wedges
345 ml (12 fl oz) olive oil
2 egg yolks, at room temperature
25 ml (1 fl oz) lemon juice
4 tablespoons pitted black olives, finely chopped
200 g (7 oz) baby rocket (arugula) leaves
1 tablespoon finely chopped fresh rosemary
4 tuna steaks (about 200 g/ 7 oz each)

1 Preheat the oven to 200°C (400°F/ Gas 6). Place the potatoes in a roasting tin and toss in 2 tablespoons of the oil. Bake for 45–50 minutes, or until crisp and golden.

2 Meanwhile, process the egg yolks in a food processor, adding 3 tablespoons of the oil drop by drop. With the motor running, pour in 185 ml (6 fl oz/¾ cup) of the oil in a thin stream until the mixture thickens and becomes creamy. With the motor still running, add 1 teaspoon of the lemon juice, season with salt and blend for 30 seconds. Stir in the olives, cover and refrigerate.

3 To make the salad, toss the rocket leaves, 2 tablespoons of the oil and 1 tablespoon of the lemon juice together in a serving bowl.

4 Press the chopped rosemary into the tuna steaks. Heat remaining tablespoon of oil in a large frying pan and sear the tuna steaks over medium–high heat for 2–3 minutes on each side, or until cooked to your liking. Serve with olive mayonnaise, potato wedges and rocket salad.

1

2

COOK'S FILE

Note: To save time, use 250 g (9 oz/ 1 cup) good-quality whole-egg mayonnaise instead of making your own.

PARMESAN CHICKEN WITH QUICK SALSA VERDE

Preparation time: 15 minutes + 10 minutes refrigeration
Cooking time: 15 minutes
Serves 4

3 eggs
30 g (1 oz/1 cup) loosely packed fresh basil
2 tablespoons capers, rinsed
1 tablespoon dijon mustard
2 tablespoons freshly grated parmesan
185 ml (6 fl oz/¾ cup) olive oil
100 g (3½ oz/1 cup) dry breadcrumbs
4 skinless, boneless chicken breasts (about 120 g/ 4¼ oz each)
150 g (5½ oz) rocket (arugula) leaves
lemon wedges, to serve

1 Place 1 egg in a saucepan of cold water, bring to the boil and cook for 1 minute. Remove and refresh under cold water. Peel, then place in a food processor with basil, capers, mustard and 1 tablespoon of the parmesan, until combined. Gradually add 3 tablespoons of the olive oil and process until you have a coarse sauce, taking care not to overprocess.

2 Beat the remaining eggs together with 1 tablespoon water. Combine the breadcrumbs with the remaining Parmesan on a plate. Pound each chicken breast between two sheets of plastic wrap with a mallet or rolling pin until 5 mm (¼ inch) thick. Dip the chicken in the egg mixture, then coat in the breadcrumb mixture. Place on a paper-lined baking tray and refrigerate for 10 minutes, or until needed.

3 Heat remaining oil in a large frying pan over high heat. Cook the chicken breasts in batches for 2–3 minutes each batch, or until golden on both sides and cooked through—keep warm between batches. Serve with the salsa verde, rocket leaves and lemon wedges.

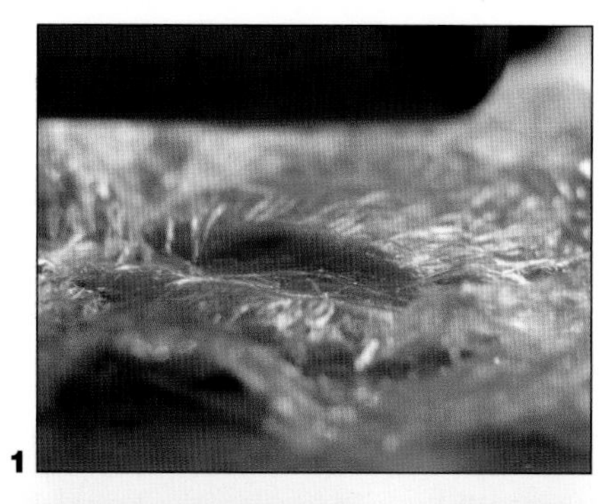
1

2

SALMON AND DILL POTATO PATTIES WITH LIME MAYONNAISE

Preparation time: 15 minutes
Cooking time: 25 minutes
Serves 4

400 g (14 oz) new potatoes (unpeeled optional), cut in half
2 teaspoons grated lime zest
310 g (11 oz/1¼ cups) good-quality whole-egg mayonnaise
425 g (15 oz) tin good-quality salmon, drained, bones removed
1 tablespoon chopped fresh dill
2 spring onions (scallions), thinly sliced
1 egg
80 g (2¾ oz/1 cup) fresh breadcrumbs
3 tablespoons oil
200 g (7 oz) rocket (arugula) leaves
lime wedges, to serve

1 Cook the potatoes in a large saucepan of boiling water for 12–15 minutes, or until tender. Drain well and cool.

2 Meanwhile, combine the zest and 250 g (9 oz/1 cup) of the mayonnaise.

3 Transfer the potato to a large bowl, then mash roughly with the back of a wooden spoon, leaving some large chunks. Stir in the salmon, dill and spring onion and season. Mix in the egg and the remaining mayonnaise. Divide into eight portions, forming palm-size patties. Press lightly into the breadcrumbs to coat.

4 Heat the oil in a non-stick frying pan and cook the patties, turning, for 3–4 minutes, or until golden brown. Drain on paper towels. Serve with a dollop of lime mayonnaise, rocket leaves and lime wedges.

1

2

CHICKEN BREASTS WITH MUSTARD CREAM SAUCE

Preparation time: 10 minutes
Cooking time: 20 minutes
Serves 4

4 skinless, boneless chicken breasts (about 200 g/ 7 oz each)
2 tablespoons oil
1 garlic clove, crushed
3 tablespoons white wine
2 tablespoons wholegrain mustard
2 teaspoons chopped fresh thyme
300 ml (10½ fl oz) cream
240 g (8½ oz) green beans, top and tailed
320 g (11¼ oz) baby yellow squash, halved

1 Pound each chicken breast between two sheets of plastic wrap with a mallet or rolling pin to about 1 cm (½ inch) thick.

2 Heat the oil in a frying pan over high heat. Add the chicken breasts and cook for 4–5 minutes on each side, or until brown. Remove and cover with foil.

3 Add the garlic to the frying pan and cook for 1 minute over medium heat, then stir in the wine, mustard and thyme. Increase the heat to medium–high and pour in the cream. Simmer for about 5 minutes, or until the sauce has reduced and thickened slightly, then season to taste.

4 Meanwhile, bring a saucepan of lightly salted water to the boil, add the beans and squash and cook for 2–4 minutes, or until just tender. Season to taste. To serve, pour a little of the sauce over the chicken and serve with the vegetables on the side

1

1

2

CHICKEN ASPARAGUS STIR-FRY

Preparation time: 15 minutes
Total cooking time: 10 minutes
Serves 4

2 tablespoons oil
1 garlic clove, crushed
10 cm (4 inch) piece fresh ginger, peeled and thinly sliced
3 skinless, boneless chicken breasts, sliced
4 spring onions (scallions), sliced
200 g (7 oz) fresh asparagus spears, sliced on the diagonal
2 tablespoons soy sauce
4 tablespoons slivered almonds, roasted

1 Heat a wok or large frying pan over high heat, add oil and swirl to coat. Add garlic, ginger and chicken, and stir-fry for 1–2 minutes, or until the chicken changes colour.
2 Add spring onion and asparagus and stir-fry for a further 2 minutes, or until the spring onion is soft.
3 Stir in soy sauce and 3 tablespoons water, cover and simmer for 2 minutes, or until the chicken is tender and the vegetables are slightly crisp. Sprinkle with almonds and serve on steamed rice or hokkien (egg) noodles.

3

CHICKEN MEATBALLS

Preparation time: 15 minutes
Total cooking time: 30 minutes
Serves 4–6

500 g (1 lb 2 oz) minced (ground) chicken
3 tablespoons fresh breadcrumbs
2 teaspoons finely chopped thyme
2 tablespoons oil
1 onion, finely chopped
2 x 425 g (15 oz) tins diced tomatoes
2 teaspoons balsamic vinegar
250 ml (9 fl oz/1 cup) chicken stock

1 Combine the chicken, breadcrumbs and thyme in a large bowl and season well. Roll a tablespoon of the mixture between your hands to make a meatball, and then repeat with the remaining mixture.

2 Heat the oil in a large frying pan and fry the meatballs in batches for 5–8 minutes, or until golden brown. Remove from the pan and drain on paper towels.

3 Add the onion to the pan and cook for 2–3 minutes, or until softened. Add the tomato, vinegar and stock, return the meatballs to the pan, then reduce the heat and simmer for 10 minutes, or until the sauce thickens and the meatballs are cooked through. Serve with pasta and garnish with basil and grated Parmesan cheese, if desired.

1

2

3

ORANGE SWEET POTATO, SPINACH AND WATER CHESTNUT STIR-FRY

Preparation time: 15 minutes
Cooking time: 20 minutes
Serves 4

300 g (10½ oz/1½ cups) long-grain rice
500 g (1 lb 2 oz) orange sweet potato
1 tablespoon oil
2 garlic cloves, crushed
2 teaspoons sambal oelek
225 g (8 oz) tin water chestnuts, sliced
2 teaspoons grated palm sugar (jaggery)
390 g (13¾ oz) English spinach, stems removed
2 tablespoons soy sauce
2 tablespoons vegetable stock

1 Bring a large saucepan of water to the boil. Add the rice and cook for 12 minutes, stirring occasionally. Drain well.
2 Meanwhile, cut the sweet potato into 1.5 cm x 1.5 cm (⅝ inch x ⅝ inch) cubes. Cook the sweet potato in a large saucepan of boiling water for 15 minutes, or until tender. Drain well.
3 Heat a wok until very hot, add the oil and swirl to coat. Stir-fry the garlic and sambal oelek for 1 minute, or until fragrant. Add the sweet potato and water chestnuts and stir-fry over medium–high heat for 2 minutes. Reduce the heat to medium, add the palm sugar and cook for a further 2 minutes, or until the sugar has melted. Add the spinach, soy sauce and stock and toss until the spinach has just wilted. Serve with the steamed rice.

COOK'S FILE

Notes: Sambal oelek is made from mashed fresh red chillies mixed with salt and vinegar or tamarind.

Palm sugar is available from most large supermarkets. Use demerara or soft brown sugar if not available.

1

LEMON GRASS BEEF

Preparation time: 15 minutes + 10 minutes marinating
Cooking time: 25 minutes
Serves 4

300 g (10½ oz/1½ cups) long-grain rice
3 garlic cloves, finely chopped
1 tablespoon grated fresh ginger
4 stems lemongrass (white part only), finely chopped
2½ tablespoons oil
600 g (1 lb 5 oz) lean rump steak, trimmed and sliced thinly across the grain
1 tablespoon lime juice
1–2 tablespoons fish sauce
2 tablespoons kecap manis
1 large red onion, cut into small wedges
200 g (7 oz) green beans, sliced on the diagonal into 5 cm (2 inch) lengths

1 Bring a large saucepan of water to the boil. Add the rice and cook for 12 minutes, stirring occasionally. Drain well.
2 Meanwhile, combine garlic, ginger, lemongrass and 2 teaspoons of oil in a non-metallic bowl. Add the beef, then marinate for 10 minutes.
3 Combine the lime juice, fish sauce and kecap manis.
4 Heat a wok until very hot, add 1 tablespoon oil and swirl to coat. Stir-fry the beef in batches for 2–3 minutes, or until browned. Remove from the wok.
5 Reheat the wok to very hot, heat the remaining oil, then add the onion and stir-fry for 2 minutes. Add the beans and cook for another 2 minutes, then return the beef to the wok. Pour in the fish sauce mixture and cook until heated through. Serve with the rice.

COOK'S FILE

Notes: Ensure your lemongrass is fresh—the end of the stalk should not be too dry and should still have a strong lemon scent.

Kecap manis is a thick sweet soy sauce available in the Asian food section of your local supermarket. If not available, use soy sauce sweetened with a little soft brown sugar.

1

FISH FILLETS WITH FENNEL AND RED CAPSICUM SALSA

Preparation time: 10 minutes
Cooking time: 20 minutes
Serves 4

750 g (1 lb 10 oz) small new potatoes
1 teaspoon fennel seeds
125 ml (4 fl oz/½ cup) olive oil
2 tablespoons drained baby capers
1 small red capsicum (pepper), deseeded and finely diced
250 g (9 oz) mixed salad leaves, washed
2 tablespoons balsamic vinegar
4 white fish fillets (blue eye cod or John Dory) (about 200 g/ 7 oz each)

1 Cook the potatoes in a large saucepan of boiling water for 15–20 minutes, or until tender. Drain and keep warm.

2 Meanwhile, to make the salsa, place the fennel seeds in a dry frying pan and dry-fry over medium heat for 1 minute, or until fragrant. Remove the seeds from the pan. Heat 1 tablespoon of the oil in the same pan over medium heat. When the oil is hot but not smoking, add the capers and flash-fry for 1–2 minutes, or until crisp. Remove from the pan. Heat another tablespoon of oil, add the capsicum and cook, stirring, for 4–5 minutes, or until cooked through. Remove from the pan and combine with the fennel seeds and fried capers.

3 Place the salad leaves in a serving bowl. To make the dressing, combine the balsamic vinegar and 3 tablespoons of the olive oil in a bowl. Add 1 tablespoon to the salsa, then toss the rest through the salad leaves.

4 Wipe the frying pan clean, then heat the remaining oil in the pan over medium–high heat. Season the fish fillets well with salt and freshly ground black pepper. When the oil is hot, but not smoking, cook the fish fillets for 2–3 minutes on each side (depending on thickness), or until cooked through. Serve the fillets immediately with the capsicum salsa potatoes and salad.

1

2

PORK WITH PAPRIKA, POTATOES AND SHALLOTS

Preparation time: 15 minutes
Cooking time: 45 minutes
Serves 4

1 tablespoon paprika
4 thick pork loin cutlets
2 tablespoons olive oil
3 tablespoons sherry vinegar
¼ teaspoon cayenne pepper
125 ml (4 fl oz/½ cup) puréed tomato
400 g (14 oz) potatoes, cut into 2 cm (¾ inch) cubes
8 French shallots, peeled
200 g (7 oz) rocket (arugula) leaves

1 Combine the paprika with ¼ teaspoon each of salt and freshly ground black pepper. Sprinkle over both sides of the pork. Heat the oil over medium heat in a deep frying pan large enough to fit the cutlets in a single layer and cook the cutlets until brown on both sides.

2 Pour the sherry vinegar into the pan and stir well to scrape up any sediment stuck to the base. Stir in the cayenne pepper, puréed tomato and 250 ml (9 fl oz/1 cup) hot water. Bring to the boil, then add the potato and shallots. Reduce the heat and simmer, covered, for 30 minutes, or until the sauce has thickened and reduced by half—check the liquid level once or twice, and add a little more water if necessary. Season.

3 To serve, divide the rocket leaves among four serving plates and place a cutlet on top. Spoon the sauce and potatoes over the top.

SWEET CHILLI STIR-FRY

Preparation time: 10 minutes
Total cooking time: 10 minutes
Serves 4–6

375 g (13 oz) hokkien (egg) noodles
4 skinless, boneless chicken thighs, cut into small pieces (see Note)
1–2 tablespoons sweet chilli sauce

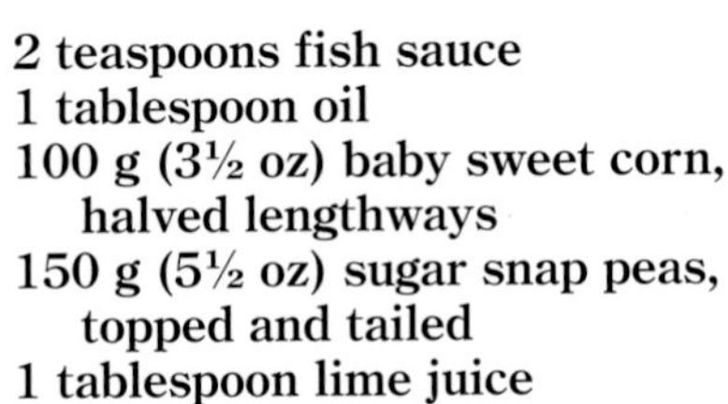

2 teaspoons fish sauce
1 tablespoon oil
100 g (3½ oz) baby sweet corn, halved lengthways
150 g (5½ oz) sugar snap peas, topped and tailed
1 tablespoon lime juice

1 Place the noodles in a large bowl, cover with boiling water and gently break apart with a fork. Leave for 5 minutes, then drain.
2 Combine the chicken, sweet chilli sauce and fish sauce in a bowl.
3 Heat a wok or frying pan over high heat, add the oil and swirl to coat. Add the chicken pieces and stir-fry for 3–5 minutes, or until cooked through. Then add the corn and sugar snap peas and stir-fry for 2 minutes. Add the noodles and lime juice and serve.

COOK'S FILE

Note: If thigh fillets are unavailable, use 3 breast fillets.

1

2

3

STEAK WITH MUSHROOM AND WINE SAUCE

Preparation time: 10 minutes
Total cooking time: 15 minutes
Serves 4

2 rump steaks, 3 cm (1¼ inches) thick
2 teaspoons butter
1 tablespoon oil
3 spring onions (scallions), finely chopped
125 g (4½ oz) button mushrooms, finely sliced
3 teaspoons cornflour (cornstarch)
250 ml (9 fl oz/1 cup) red wine
3 tablespoons chopped parsley

1

2

1 Trim all fat from steaks; cut each steak in half. Heat butter and oil in a heavy-based frying pan. Cook steaks over high heat for minutes; turn over and cook for another 2 minutes or until done to your liking. Remove steaks from pan, cover and keep warm. Add spring onion to pan, stir for 3 minutes, add mushrooms and stir for 3 minutes or until mushrooms are soft.

2 Combine cornflour with 2 tablespoons of the wine to form a smooth paste. Stir into remaining wine and add all at once to the mushroom mixture. Cook until mixture boils and thickens. Stir in parsley.

3 Place steaks on serving dishes. Spoon sauce over fillets; serve immediately. Serve with salad greens or steamed vegetables.

SEARED SALMON WITH SESAME AND CUCUMBER NOODLES

Preparation time: 15 minutes + 2 hours refrigeration
Cooking time: 10 minutes
Serves 4

250 g (9 oz) buckwheat soba noodles
1½ tablespoons sesame oil
2 tablespoons kecap manis
1 tablespoon Chinese black vinegar
2 Lebanese (short) cucumbers, thinly sliced
6 spring onions (scallions), trimmed and sliced on the diagonal into 4 cm (1½ inch) lengths
2 tablespoons black sesame seeds
600 g (1 lb 5 oz) salmon fillet pieces, skinned and boned

1 Cook the noodles in a large saucepan of boiling water according to the packet instructions until tender—this should take about 5 minutes. Drain well. Place in a large bowl and mix in 2 teaspoons of the sesame oil, then set aside to cool. Combine the kecap manis, vinegar and the remaining sesame oil, then toss 1 tablespoon of the mixture through the noodles. Cover the noodles and refrigerate for about 2 hours.

2 About 20 minutes before serving, remove the noodles from the refrigerator and gently mix in the cucumber, spring onion and black sesame seeds.

3 Heat a large frying pan over medium–high heat. Brush the salmon pieces lightly with oil and season with salt and freshly ground black pepper. Cook for 1–2 minutes on each side, or until cooked to your liking. Remove from the heat and allow to cool until cool enough to handle. Flake the fish into large pieces and gently incorporate it into the noodles, along with the rest of the dressing—be careful not to over-handle or the salmon will flake into small pieces. Serve immediately.

1

2

PRAWNS WITH SPICY TAMARIND SAUCE

Preparation time: 15 minutes
Cooking time: 25 minutes
Serves 4

80 g (2¾ oz/½ cup) raw cashew nuts
250 g (9 oz/1¼ cups) jasmine rice
2 garlic cloves, finely chopped
1½ tablespoons fish sauce
1 tablespoon sambal oelek
1 tablespoon peanut oil
1 kg (2 lb 4 oz) raw medium prawns (shrimp), peeled and deveined with tails intact
2 teaspoons tamarind concentrate
1½ tablespoons grated palm sugar (jaggery)
350 g (12 oz) choy sum, cut into 10 cm (4 inch) lengths

1 Preheat the oven to 180°C (350°F/Gas 4). Spread the cashews on a baking tray and bake for 5–8 minutes, or until lightly golden—watch carefully as they will burn easily.
2 Meanwhile, bring a large saucepan of water to the boil. Add the rice and cook for 12 minutes, stirring occasionally. Drain well.
3 Place the garlic, fish sauce, sambal oelek and toasted cashews in a blender or food processor, adding 2–3 tablespoons of water, if needed, and blend to a rough paste.
4 Heat a wok until very hot, add the oil and swirl to coat. Add the prawns, toss for 1–2 minutes, or until starting to turn pink. Remove from the wok. Add the cashew paste and stir-fry for 1 minute, or until it starts to brown slightly. Add the tamarind, sugar and about 4 tablespoons water, then bring to the boil, stirring well.
5 Return the prawns to the wok and stir to coat. Cook for 2–3 minutes, or until the prawns are cooked through.
6 Place the choy sum in a paper-lined bamboo steamer and steam over a wok or saucepan of simmering water for 3 minutes, or until tender. Serve with the prawns and rice.

COOK'S FILE

Note: To save time, you can purchase pre-peeled raw prawns with the tails intact. You will only need 500 g (1 lb 2 oz) as the shells make up roughly half the weight of the prawns.

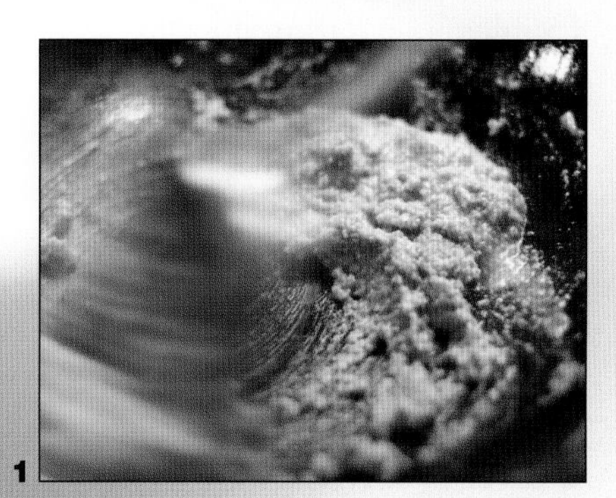

1

LAMB BACKSTRAPS WITH SPICED LENTILS AND MINT RAITA

Preparation time: 15 minutes + 10 minutes marinating
Cooking time: 20 minutes
Serves 4

125 g (4½ oz/½ cup) plain yoghurt
2 tablespoons finely chopped fresh mint
1 tablespoon garam masala
3 teaspoons ground cumin
½ teaspoon chilli powder
4 tablespoons oil
4 lamb backstraps (about 150 g/ 5½ oz) each)
2 teaspoons grated fresh ginger
1 teaspoon ground turmeric
2 x 425 g (15 oz) tins lentils, drained and rinsed

1 Combine the yoghurt and half the mint in a small non-metallic bowl. Cover and set aside.

2 Place the garam masala in a small dry frying pan and dry-fry over medium heat for 1 minute, or until fragrant. Remove from the pan, then repeat with the ground cumin. Combine the chilli, 2 teaspoons of the garam masala, 2 teaspoons of the cumin and 2 tablespoons of the oil. Place the lamb in a non-metallic dish and brush with the spiced oil. Cover and marinate for at least 10 minutes, or overnight, if time permits.

3 Meanwhile, heat 1 tablespoon of the remaining oil in a saucepan. Add the ginger, turmeric and remaining cumin and cook for 30 seconds, or until fragrant. Add the lentils and stir thoroughly until heated through. Reduce the heat to low, add the remaining garam masala and season well with salt. Cook, covered, for 5 minutes, adding 3 tablespoons water if the lentils start to stick. Before serving, stir in the remaining mint.

4 Heat a large frying pan over medium–high heat and add the remaining oil. Add the backstraps and cook for 3–4 minutes each side for medium–rare, or until cooked to your liking. Allow to rest for several minutes, then cut into 1 cm (½ inch) slices on the diagonal.

5 To serve, place a small mound of lentils on a plate, arrange the lamb slices on top and serve with a dollop of the minted yoghurt. Garnish with fresh mint, if desired.

1

2

BEEF STROGANOFF

Preparation time: 15 minutes
Cooking time: 20 minutes
Serves 4

600 g (1 lb 5 oz) rib eye fillet or rump
3 tablespoons seasoned plain (all-purpose) flour
375 g (13 oz) fettucine or tagliatelle
60 g (2¼ oz) butter
1 small onion, finely chopped
300 g (10½ oz) button mushrooms, thickly sliced
1 tablespoon tomato paste (concentrated purée)
3 tablespoons red wine
300 ml (10½ fl oz) cream

1 Pound the slices of beef between two sheets of plastic wrap with a mallet or rolling pin until half their thickness. Cut each slice into strips about 1 cm (½ inch) wide. Place in a plastic bag with the seasoned flour and shake to coat.

2 Bring a large saucepan of water to the boil and cook the fettucine according to the packet instructions, until al dente.

3 Meanwhile, melt 40 g (1½ oz) of the butter in a frying pan over medium heat and cook the onion for 2 minutes. Add the beef in batches and cook for 5 minutes, or until evenly browned.

4 Remove beef from the pan and keep warm. Heat the remaining butter in the pan and add the mushrooms, stirring, for 2–3 minutes, or until soft and lightly browned. Add the tomato paste and the red wine, stirring continuously for 2 minutes, or until the sauce has reduced. Add the beef, stir in the cream, then reduce the heat to medium–low and simmer gently for a further minute, or until the sauce has thickened. Serve with the fettucine or tagliatelle.

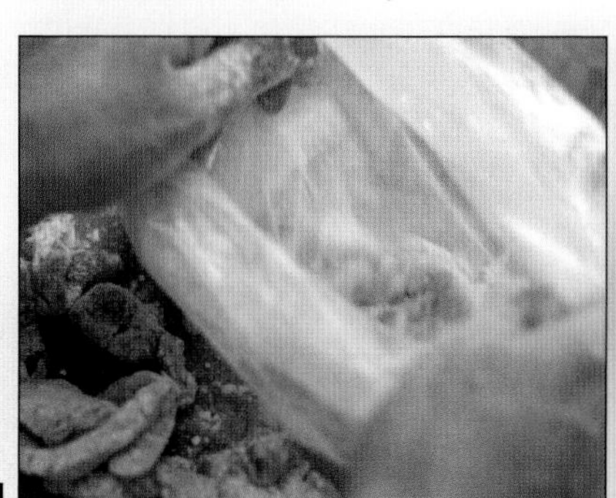

1

2

SPRING ONION LAMB

Preparation time: 10 minutes + 10 minutes marinating
Cooking time: 30 minutes
Serves 4

600 g (1 lb 5 oz) lean lamb backstraps
1 tablespoon Chinese rice wine (see Note) or dry sherry
3 tablespoons soy sauce
½ teaspoon white pepper
½ teaspoon salt
6 spring onions (scallions)
300 g (10½ oz/1½ cups) long-grain rice
2 tablespoons oil
750 g (1 lb 10 oz) choy sum, cut into 10 cm (4 inch) lengths
3 garlic cloves, crushed
1 tablespoon Chinese black vinegar (see Note)
1 teaspoon sesame oil

1

1 Slice the lamb backstrap across the grain into very thin slices. Place in a non-metallic bowl with the rice wine, 1 tablespoon of the soy sauce, salt and pepper, and mix well. Cover and refrigerate for 10 minutes. Slice the spring onions diagonally into 4 cm (1½ inch) lengths.

2 Meanwhile, bring a large saucepan of water to the boil. Add the rice and cook for 12 minutes, stirring occasionally. Drain.

3 Heat a wok over high heat, add ½ tablespoon oil and swirl to coat. Add the choy sum, stir-fry quickly, then add 1 clove of the crushed garlic and 1 tablespoon soy sauce. Cook for 3 minutes, or until cooked, but crisp. Immediately take the wok off the heat, remove the greens and keep warm.

4 Wipe the wok clean and heat over high heat, then add 1 tablespoon oil and swirl to coat. Add the lamb in two batches and stir-fry quickly over high heat for 1–2 minutes, or until brown. Remove from the wok.

5 Add a little more oil to the wok, if necessary. Add the spring onion and remaining garlic and stir-fry for 1–2 minutes. Combine the vinegar, sesame oil and the remaining soy sauce. Pour into the wok, stirring for 1 minute, or until combined. Return the lamb to the wok and continue to stir-fry for another minute, or until combined and heated through. Serve immediately with the stir-fried greens and rice.

COOK'S FILE

Note: Chinese rice wine and Chinese black vinegar are available in Asian grocery stores.

1

2

GINGER CHICKEN STIR-FRY WITH HOKKIEN NOODLES

Preparation time: 15 minutes + 5 minutes soaking
Cooking time: 10 minutes
Serves 4

2½ tablespoons finely shredded fresh ginger
3 tablespoons mirin
2 tablespoons soy sauce
600 g (1 lb 5 oz) skinless, boneless chicken tenderloins or chicken breasts, cut diagonally into thin strips
180 g (6 oz) fresh baby corn
350 g (12 oz) choy sum
150 g (5½ oz) fresh oyster mushrooms
500 g (1 lb 2 oz) Hokkien noodles, gently separated
2 tablespoons oil
2 tablespoons oyster sauce

1 Combine the ginger, mirin and soy sauce in a non-metallic bowl. Add the chicken, coat well, then marinate while preparing the vegetables.

2 Cut the corn in half lengthways; trim the ends off the choy sum and cut into 6 cm (2½ inch) lengths. If the mushrooms are very large, cut them in half. Soak the noodles in a large heatproof bowl in boiling water for 5 minutes. Drain and refresh under cold running water.

3 Heat a wok until very hot, add 1 tablespoon of the oil and swirl to coat. Remove the chicken from the marinade with a slotted spoon and cook in two batches over very high heat for 2 minutes, or until brown and just cooked. Remove from the wok.

4 Add the remaining oil to the wok and stir-fry the mushrooms and corn for 1–2 minutes, or until just softened. Add the remaining marinade, bring to the boil, then add the chicken, choy sum and noodles. Stir in the oyster sauce and cook, tossing well, for 1–2 minutes, or until the choy sum has wilted slightly and the noodles are warmed through.

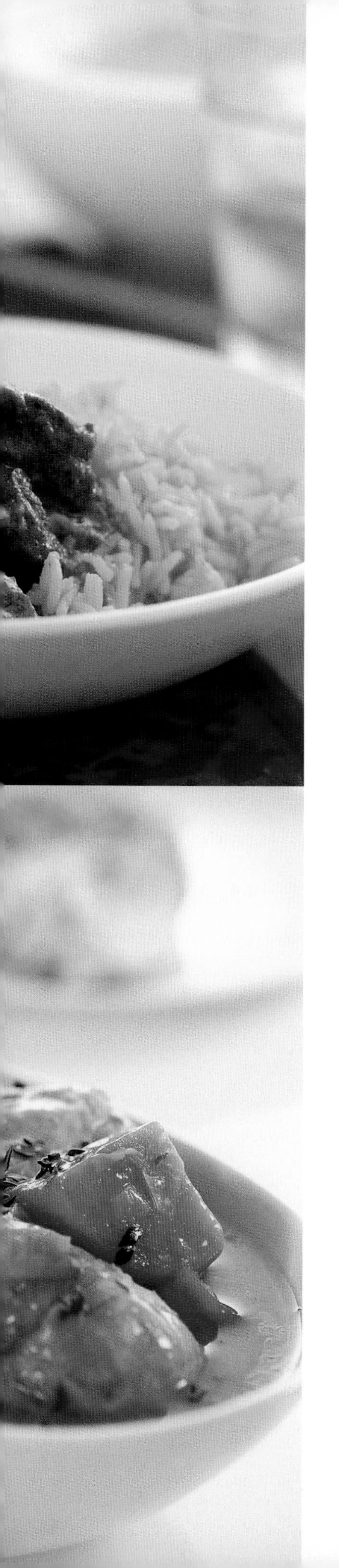

Easy stews and casseroles

CHICKEN, ARTICHOKE AND BROAD BEAN STEW

Preparation time: 15 minutes
Cooking time: 1 hour 25 minutes
Serves 4

155 g (5½ oz/1 cup) frozen broad (fava) beans
8 chicken thighs on the bone (skin removed, optional)
60 g (2¼ oz/½ cup) seasoned plain (all-purpose) flour
2 tablespoons oil
1 large red onion, cut into small wedges
125 ml (4 fl oz/½ cup) dry white wine
310 ml (10¾ fl oz/1¼ cups) chicken stock
2 teaspoons finely chopped fresh rosemary
340 g (12 oz) marinated artichokes, well drained and quartered
800 g (1 lb 12 oz) potatoes, cut into large cubes
60 g (2¼ oz) butter

1 Remove the skins from the broad beans. Coat chicken in the flour, shaking off the excess. Heat the oil in a saucepan or flameproof casserole dish, then brown the chicken in two batches on all sides over medium heat. Remove and drain on paper towel.

2 Add the onion to the pan and cook for 3–4 minutes, or until soft but not brown. Increase the heat to high, pour in the wine and boil for 2 minutes, or until reduced to a syrup. Stir in 250 ml (9 fl oz/1 cup) of the stock and bring just to the boil, then return the chicken to the pan with the rosemary. Reduce the heat to low and simmer, covered, for 45 minutes.

3 Add artichokes to the pan, increase the heat to high and return to the boil. Reduce to a simmer and cook, uncovered, for 10–15 minutes. Add beans and cook for a further 5 minutes.

4 Meanwhile, cook the potatoes in a saucepan of boiling water for 15–20 minutes, or until tender. Drain, then return to the pan. Add the butter and the remaining stock and mash with a potato masher. Serve on the side of the stew.

1

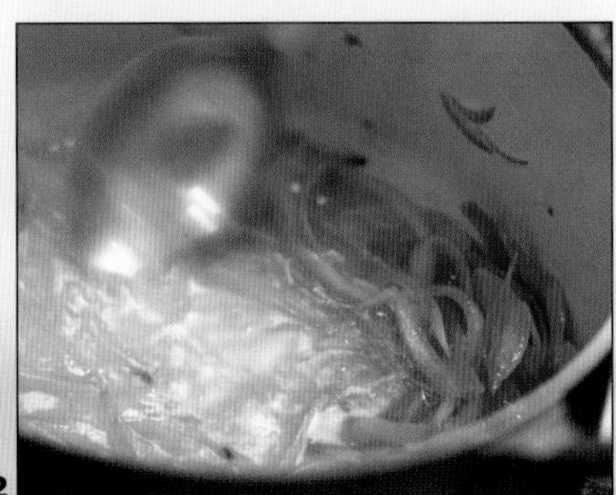
2

3

PAPRIKA VEAL WITH CARAWAY PASTA

Preparation time: 10 minutes
Cooking time: 1 hour 35 minutes
Serves 4

3 tablespoons oil
1 kg (2 lb 4 oz) veal shoulder, diced
1 large onion, thinly sliced
3 garlic cloves, finely chopped
3 tablespoons Hungarian paprika
½ teaspoon caraway seeds
2 x 400 g (14 oz) tins chopped tomatoes, one drained
350 g (12 oz) fresh fettucine
40 g (1½ oz) butter, softened

1 Heat half the oil in a large saucepan over medium–high heat, then brown the veal in batches for 3 minutes per batch. Remove the veal from the pan and set aside with any pan juices.

2 Add the remaining oil to the pan and sauté the onion and garlic over medium heat for 5 minutes, or until softened. Add the paprika and ¼ teaspoon of the caraway seeds and stir for 30 seconds.

3 Add the chopped tomatoes and their liquid plus 125 ml (4 fl oz/½ cup) water. Return the veal to the pan with any juices, increase the heat to high and bring to the boil. Reduce the heat to low, then cover and simmer for 1 hour 15 minutes, or until the meat is tender and the sauce has thickened.

4 About 15 minutes before the veal is ready, cook the pasta in a large saucepan of boiling salted water according to the packet instructions until al dente. Drain, then return to the pan. Stir in the butter and the remaining caraway seeds. Serve immediately with the paprika veal.

1

2

BEEF AND RED WINE STEW

Preparation time: 10 minutes
Cooking time: 2 hours
Serves 4

1 kg (2 lb 4 oz) diced beef
3 tablespoons seasoned plain (all-purpose) flour
1 tablespoon oil
150 g (5½ oz) bacon, diced
8 bulb spring onions (scallions), greens trimmed to 2 cm (¾ inch)
200 g (7 oz) button mushrooms
500 ml (17 fl oz/2 cups) red wine
2 tablespoons tomato paste (concentrated purée)
500 ml (17 fl oz/2 cups) beef stock
1 bouquet garni (see Note)

1 Toss the beef in the seasoned flour until evenly coated, shaking off any excess. Heat the oil in a large saucepan over high heat. Cook the beef in three batches for about 3 minutes, or until well browned, adding a little extra oil as needed. Remove from the pan.
2 Add the bacon to the pan and cook for 2 minutes, or until browned. Remove with a slotted spoon and add to the beef. Add the spring onions and mushrooms and cook for 5 minutes, or until the onions are browned. Remove.
3 Slowly pour the red wine into the pan, scraping up any sediment from the bottom with a wooden spoon. Stir in the tomato paste and stock. Add the bouquet garni and return the beef, bacon and any juices. Bring to the boil, then reduce the heat and simmer for 45 minutes, then return the spring onions and mushrooms to the pan. Cook for 1 hour, or until the meat is very tender and the sauce is glossy. Serve with steamed new potatoes or mash.

COOK'S FILE

Note: To make a bouquet garni, wrap the green part of a leek around a bay leaf, a sprig of thyme, a sprig of parsley and celery leaves, and tie with string. The combination of herbs can be varied according to taste.

1

2

THAI GREEN CHICKEN CURRY WITH CORIANDER RICE

Preparation time: 10 minutes
Cooking time: 20 minutes
Serves 4

250 g (9 oz/1¼ cups) jasmine rice
1 tablespoon vegetable oil
1–2 tablespoons good-quality Thai green curry paste
4 fresh mahrut (kaffir lime) leaves
1 tablespoon fish sauce
2 teaspoons palm sugar (jaggery)
400 ml (14 fl oz) tin coconut cream
750 g (1 lb 10 oz) skinless, boneless chicken breasts, cut into strips
4 tablespoons roughly chopped fresh coriander (cilantro) leaves
2 tablespoons whole coriander (cilantro) leaves

1 Bring a large saucepan of water to the boil. Add the rice and cook for 12 minutes, stirring occasionally. Drain well.

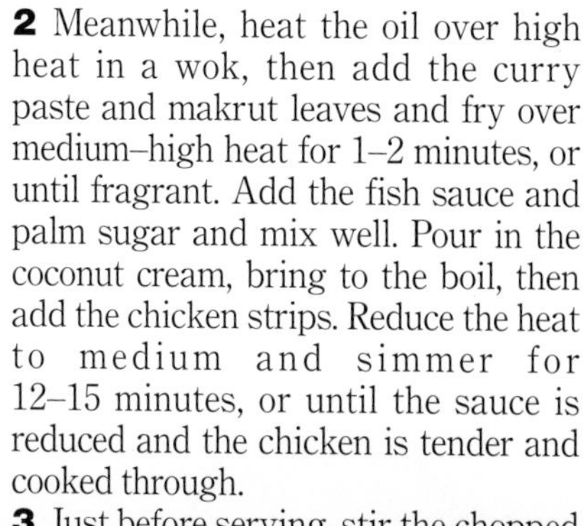

2 Meanwhile, heat the oil over high heat in a wok, then add the curry paste and makrut leaves and fry over medium–high heat for 1–2 minutes, or until fragrant. Add the fish sauce and palm sugar and mix well. Pour in the coconut cream, bring to the boil, then add the chicken strips. Reduce the heat to medium and simmer for 12–15 minutes, or until the sauce is reduced and the chicken is tender and cooked through.

3 Just before serving, stir the chopped coriander through the rice. Serve the curry over the coriander rice, garnished with a few whole coriander leaves.

1

2

MIXED VEGETABLE CURRY

Preparation time: 10 minutes
Total cooking time: 25 minutes
Serves 4

1 tablespoon oil
1 onion, sliced
500 g (1 lb 2 oz) baby potatoes, quartered
250 g (9 oz) broccoli florets
2 large carrots, sliced
425 g (15 oz) tin tomatoes
3 teaspoons curry paste
500 ml (17 fl oz/2 cups) coconut milk
250 g (9 oz) small button mushrooms, halved

1 Heat oil in a large pan and add sliced onion. Stir over medium heat for 3–5 minutes or until golden. Add potato, broccoli, carrot, undrained, crushed tomato and curry paste; stir to combine. Add coconut milk to pan; bring to the boil. Reduce heat to low, simmer, uncovered, for 15 minutes or until vegetables are almost tender.

2 Add mushrooms and cook for another 5 minutes or until vegetables are tender.

1

2

CHICKEN PROVENCALE

Preparation time: 15 minutes
Total cooking time: 1 hour 20 minutes
Serves 4–6

1 tablespoon olive oil
1.5 kg (3 lb 5 oz) chicken drumsticks
1 onion, chopped
1 red capsicum (pepper), chopped
4 tablespoons white wine
4 tablespoons chicken stock
425 g (15 oz) tin chopped tomatoes
2 tablespoons tomato paste (concentrated purée)
90 g (3¼ oz/½ cup) black olives
4 tablespoons shredded basil

1 Heat the oil in a saucepan over high heat, add the chicken, in batches, and cook for 3–4 minutes, or until browned. Return all the chicken to the pan and add the onion and capsicum. Cook for 2–3 minutes, or until the onion is soft.

2 Add the wine, stock, tomatoes, tomato paste and olives, and bring to the boil. Reduce the heat, cover and simmer for 30 minutes. Remove the lid, turn the chicken pieces over and cook for another 30 minutes, or until the chicken is tender and the cooking liquid has thickened. Season to taste with salt, black pepper and a little sugar, if desired. Sprinkle with the basil and serve with boiled rice.

1

2

BEEF MASALA WITH COCONUT RICE

Preparation time: 15 minutes + 10 minutes standing
Cooking time: 1 hour 50 minutes
Serves 4

1 tablespoon oil
1 kg (2 lb 4 oz) chuck beef, trimmed and cut into 2 cm (¾ inch) cubes
1 large onion, thinly sliced
3 garlic cloves, chopped
4 tablespoons tikka masala curry paste
2 teaspoons tamarind concentrate
2 x 400 ml (14 fl oz) tins coconut milk
4 fresh curry leaves
300 g (10½ oz/1½ cups) jasmine rice

1 To make the beef masala, heat the oil in a large saucepan over high heat. Add the meat and cook in three batches, for 4 minutes per batch, or until evenly browned. Remove from the pan.

2 Reduce the heat to medium, add the onion and cook for 5 minutes. Add the garlic and cook for 1 minute. Stir in the curry paste and tamarind and cook for 30–60 seconds, or until fragrant. Return the beef to the pan, add 550 ml (19 fl oz) coconut milk and the curry leaves and bring to the boil. Reduce the heat and simmer gently for 1 hour 30 minutes, or until the meat is tender and the sauce has reduced. Check occasionally to ensure that the sauce doesn't stick to the bottom of the pan—add some water if necessary.

3 Meanwhile, to make the coconut rice, wash and thoroughly drain the rice. Place the rice, the remaining coconut milk and 250 ml (9 fl oz/1 cup) water in a saucepan. Bring slowly to the boil, stirring constantly, and boil for 1 minute. Reduce the heat to low and cook, covered tightly, for 20 minutes. Remove from the heat and leave, covered, for 10 minutes. Fluff the rice with a fork before serving. To serve, season the curry to taste, remove the curry leaves, if desired, and serve with the rice.

1

CHICKEN AND CIDER STEW WITH APPLE AND POTATO MASH

Preparation time: 15 minutes
Cooking time: 55 minutes
Serves 4

1 kg (2 lb 4 oz) skinless, boneless chicken thighs, trimmed and cut into 2 cm (¾ inch) cubes
1½ tablespoons finely chopped fresh thyme
1 tablespoon oil
90 g (3¼ oz) butter
3 French shallots, thinly sliced
375 ml (13 fl oz/1½ cups) apple cider
1 kg (2 lb 4 oz) potatoes, cubed
2 large green apples, peeled, cored and sliced into eighths
170 ml (5½ fl oz/⅔ cup) cream

1 Season the chicken thighs with 2 teaspoons of the thyme and salt and black pepper. Heat the oil and 20 g (1 tablespoon) of the butter in.a large saucepan over medium–high heat. Cook the chicken in two batches for 2–3 minutes, or until evenly browned. Remove from the pan.

2 Add French shallots and remaining thyme to the pan and sauté for 2 minutes. Pour in the cider, then bring to the boil, scraping off any sediment that has stuck to the bottom of the pan. Return the chicken to the pan and cover. Reduce the heat to medium–low and cook for 35–40 minutes, or until the chicken is tender and the sauce has reduced (check occasionally to see if any water needs to be added).

3 Meanwhile, cook the potato and apple in a saucepan of boiling water for 15–20 minutes, or until tender. Drain and return to the pan over low heat for a minute to allow any water to evaporate. Remove from the heat, and mash with a potato masher. Stir in 2 tablespoons of the cream and the remaining butter with a wooden spoon, then season well.

4 Gently stir the remaining cream into the chicken stew and cook for a further 2–4 minutes, or until the sauce has thickened. Serve at once with the potato and apple mash and a crisp green salad.

1

2

3

LEAN PORK STEW WITH ASIAN FLAVOURS

Preparation time: 20 minutes
Total cooking time: 50 minutes
Serves 4

2 teaspoons oil
2 garlic cloves, crushed
1 tablespoon thinly sliced fresh ginger
1 teaspoon Sichuan pepper, crushed
1 star anise
800 g (1 lb 12 oz) pork fillet, cut into 3 cm (1¼ inch) cubes
250 ml (9 fl oz/1 cup) chicken stock
1 tablespoon light soy sauce
1 tablespoon cornflour (cornstarch)
2 teaspoons chilli bean paste
250 g (9 oz) Chinese broccoli (gai lan) cut into 4 cm (1½ inch) lengths

1 Heat the oil in a heavy-based saucepan over high heat. Add the garlic, ginger, Sichuan pepper and star anise and cook for 30 seconds, or until fragrant. Stir in the pork to coat.
2 Add the stock, soy sauce and 250 ml (9 fl oz/1 cup) water and bring to the boil. Reduce the heat and simmer for 40 minutes, or until the pork is tender. Combine the cornflour with 2 tablespoons of cooking liquid. Stir until smooth. Add to the pan and stir over medium heat for 3–4 minutes, or until the mixture thickens slightly.
3 Stir in the bean paste and Chinese broccoli and cook for a further 2 minutes, or until the broccoli is just tender. Serve with steamed rice.

Crush the Sichuan pepper in a mortar and pestle.

Cut the Chinese broccoli into short lengths, using a sharp knife.

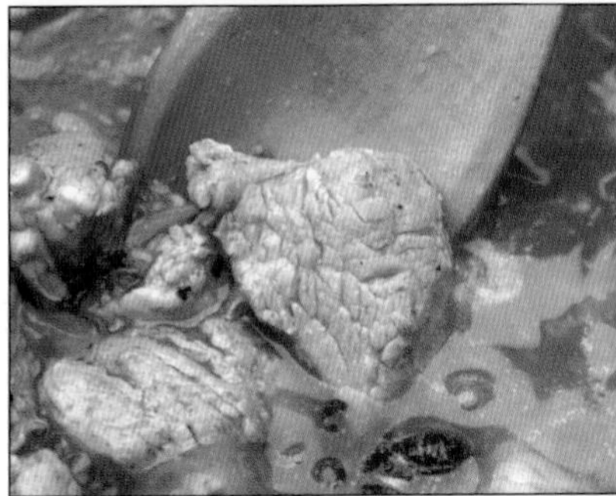

Stir the cornflour mixture into the stew until the mixture thickens slightly.

BRAISED LAMB SHANKS IN RICH TOMATO SAUCE ON POLENTA

Preparation time: 10 minutes
Cooking time: 2 hours 30 minutes
Serves 4

2 tablespoons olive oil
1 large red onion, sliced
4 French-trimmed lamb shanks (about 250 g/9 oz each)
2 garlic cloves, crushed
400 g (14 oz) tin peeled chopped tomatoes
125 ml (4 fl oz/½ cup) red wine
2 teaspoons chopped fresh rosemary
150 g (5½ oz/1 cup) instant polenta (cornmeal)
50 g (1¾ oz) butter
50 g (1¾ oz/½ cup) grated parmesan

1

1 Preheat the oven to warm 160°C (315°F/Gas 2–3). Heat the oil in a 4 litre (16 cup) flameproof casserole dish over medium heat and sauté the onion for 3–4 minutes, or until softening and becoming transparent. Add the lamb shanks and cook for 2–3 minutes, or until lightly browned. Add the garlic, tomato and wine, then bring to the boil and cook for 3–4 minutes. Stir in the rosemary. Season with ¼ teaspoon each of salt and pepper.

2 Cover, transfer to the oven and cook for 2 hours. Remove the lid, return to the oven and simmer for a further 15 minutes, or until the lamb just starts to fall off the bone. Check periodically that the sauce is not too dry, adding water if needed.

3 About 20 minutes before serving, bring 1 litre (4 cups) water to the boil in a saucepan. Add the polenta in a thin stream, whisking continuously, then reduce the heat to very low. Simmer for 8–10 minutes, or until thick and coming away from the side of the saucepan. Stir in the butter and parmesan. To serve, spoon the polenta onto serving plates, top with the shanks and a little sauce from the casserole over the shanks.

BEEF CURRY WITH FRESH HERBS

Preparation time: 10 minutes
Total cooking time: 1 hour 45 minutes
Serves 4

1 tablespoon oil
600 g (1 lb 5 oz) round steak, cut into cubes
2 onions, chopped
1 tablespoon curry paste
500 ml (17 fl oz/2 cups) water or beef stock
2 tablespoons chopped mint
2 tablespoons chopped coriander (cilantro)
4 tablespoons plain yoghurt

1 Heat oil in heavy-based pan. Add beef cubes, cook in batches over medium–high heat for 2 minutes or until well browned on all sides. Return all meat to pan.

2 Add onion, stir for 2 minutes or until brown. Add curry paste, stir for 1 minute. Add water or beef stock, bring to the boil. Reduce heat to low and cook, covered, 1–1½ hours or until meat is tender and liquid is reduced and thickened. Stir occasionally during cooking. Add chopped mint, coriander and yoghurt; stir until combined. Garnish with a sprig of fresh herbs, if desired.

COOK'S FILE

Storage time: Curry can be cooked up to 3 days before required. Store, covered; in refrigerator.

1

2

CHICKEN WITH CAPSICUM AND GARLIC

Preparation time: 10 minutes
Total cooking time: 25 minutes
Serves 4

3 tablespoons olive oil
8 skinless, boneless chicken thighs, halved
2 onions, sliced
6 garlic cloves, crushed
4 bacon rashers, sliced
2 red capsicums (peppers), sliced
425 g (15 oz) tin tomatoes
3 tablespoons chicken stock

Heat oil in pan; add chicken in single layer. Cook over medium–high heat for 3 minutes each side or until golden. Remove from pan and drain on paper towel. Add onion, garlic and bacon to the pan. Cook, stirring, for 3–5 minutes or until golden. Add capsicum, cook for another 3 minutes, stirring occasionally.

1 Add undrained, crushed tomato and stock to pan; bring to the boil. Reduce heat to low. Return chicken to pan and simmer, covered, for 15 minutes or until chicken is tender, stirring occasionally. Season with salt and pepper. Serve.

COOK'S FILE

Variation: Use 2 slices of prosciutto instead of bacon.

1

2

MOROCCAN CHICKEN

Preparation time: 10 minutes +
5 minutes standing
Cooking time: 35 minutes
Serves 4

1 tablespoon Moroccan spice
800 g (1 lb 12 oz) boneless chicken thighs, trimmed and halved
1 tablespoon oil
60 g (2¼ oz) butter
1 large onion, cut into wedges
1 cinnamon stick
2 garlic cloves, crushed
2 tablespoons lemon juice plus wedges, to serve
250 ml (9 fl oz/1 cup) chicken stock
4 tablespoons pitted prunes, halved
225 g (8 oz/1½ cups) couscous

1 Sprinkle half the spice blend over the chicken. Heat the oil and 1 tablespoon of the butter in a large saucepan or deep-sided frying pan over medium heat. Cook the chicken in batches for 5 minutes, or until evenly browned. Remove from the pan, then add the onion and cinnamon stick and cook for 2–3 minutes before adding the garlic. Return the chicken to the pan and add the lemon juice and the remaining spice mix. Season to taste, then cook, covered, for 5 minutes.

2 Add the stock and prunes to the pan and bring to the boil. Reduce the heat to medium–low and cook, uncovered, for 15 minutes, or until the chicken is cooked and the liquid has reduced to a sauce. Before serving, stir 1 tablespoon of the butter into the sauce.

3 About 10 minutes before the chicken is ready, place the couscous in a heatproof bowl, add 375 ml (13 fl oz/1½ cups) boiling water, and stand for 3–5 minutes. Stir in the remaining butter and fluff with a fork until the butter has melted and the grains separate. Serve with the chicken.

COOK'S FILE

Note: Depending on the quality and freshness of the Moroccan spice blend you buy, you may need to use a little more then specified in the recipe.

1

VEGETABLE TAGINE WITH COUSCOUS

Preparation time: 15 minutes + 5 minutes standing
Cooking time: 40 minutes
Serves 4

3 tablespoons olive oil
1 large red capsicum (pepper), deseeded and cut into quarters
1 large eggplant (aubergine), sliced into 1 cm (½ inch) rounds, then in half again
400 g (14 oz) tin chopped tomatoes
1 tablespoon harissa paste (see Note)
1 tablespoon Moroccan spice blend
250 ml (9 fl oz/1 cup) vegetable stock
2 large zucchini (courgettes), cut into 2 cm (¾ inch) chunks
225 g (8 oz/1½ cups) couscous
1 tablespoons butter

1 Heat 1 tablespoon of the oil in a saucepan over medium–high heat. Sauté the capsicum, skin-side-down, covered, for 3–4 minutes, or until the skin is well browned. Remove from the pan. Peel off the skin and cut the flesh into 1 cm (½ inch) slices. Heat the remaining oil in the pan and cook the eggplant in batches over medium–high heat for 4–5 minutes, or until well browned. Remove.

2 Return the capsicum to the pan, then stir in the tomato, harissa paste and Moroccan spice blend. Pour in the stock and bring to the boil. Reduce the heat to medium–low and simmer, uncovered, for 15 minutes. Add the zucchini and eggplant and cook for a further 8 minutes, or until the vegetables are tender.

3 About 10 minutes before the vegetables are ready, place the couscous in a heatproof bowl, add 375 ml (13 fl oz/1½ cups) boiling water, and leave for 3–5 minutes. Stir in the butter and fluff with a fork until the butter has melted and the grains separate. Serve the vegetable tagine with the couscous.

COOK'S FILE

Note: Harissa is a blend of chillies, garlic, spices and oil available at delicatessens or specialist food stores.

1

CHICKEN, LEEK AND SWEET POTATO ONE POT

Preparation time: 15 minutes
Total cooking time: 1 hour 40 minutes
Serves 4

2 tablespoons olive oil
1.5 kg (3 lb 5 oz) chicken pieces, on the bone
1 leek, cut into 2 cm (¾ inch) slices
2 garlic cloves, crushed
2 tablespoons plain (all-purpose) flour
500 ml (17 fl oz/2 cups) chicken stock
600 g (1 lb 5 oz) orange sweet potato, peeled chopped
2 tablespoons thyme

1 Preheat the oven to 220°C (425°F/Gas 7). Heat 1 tablespoon of the oil in a large ovenproof casserole dish, add the chicken, in batches, and cook for 3–4 minutes, or until browned. Set aside. Add the remaining oil and cook the leek and garlic for 2 minutes, or until soft.

2 Add the flour to the dish and cook, stirring, for about 1 minute to brown the flour. Gradually add the stock, stirring until the sauce boils and thickens. Remove from the heat. Return the chicken to the pan.

3 Add the sweet potato and half the thyme. Cover the casserole and bake for 1½ hours, or until the chicken is cooked and the sweet potato is tender. Season and scatter with the remaining thyme. Serve with steamed rice.

1

2

3

CHICKEN, MUSHROOM AND BROWN LENTIL CASSEROLE

Preparation time: 10 minutes
Total cooking time: 1 hour
Serves 4

50 g (1¾ oz) butter
180 g (6 oz) button mushrooms, sliced
4 chicken 'lovely legs' and 4 skinless thigh cutlets (see Note)
2 teaspoons cumin seeds
6 spring onions (scallions), sliced
500 ml (17 fl oz/2 cups) chicken stock
140 g (5 oz/¾ cup) brown lentils
2 tablespoons kecap manis
4 Roma (plum tomatoes)

1 Melt half the butter in a frying pan and quickly cook the mushrooms for 2–3 minutes, or until softened, then remove from the pan.

2 Melt the remaining butter, add the chicken and cook for 3–4 minutes each side, or until brown. Add the cumin seeds and half the spring onion and cook for 1 minute. Add the stock and lentils and combine, making sure all the lentils are submerged. Bring to the boil, then reduce the heat and simmer, covered, for 30 minutes. Remove the lid and turn the chicken over, again making sure all the lentils are covered. Increase the heat and cook for a further 20 minutes, uncovered, allowing the stock to reduce. Check that the chicken is cooked and the lentils are tender.

3 Stir through the kecap manis and the mushrooms, and season with salt and black pepper. Scatter with the remaining spring onions and serve with seared Roma (plum) tomatoes.

COOK'S FILE

Note: 'Lovely legs' are drumsticks with the skin and lower leg bone removed.

1

2

3

1

2

COCONUT BEEF CURRY ON TURMERIC RICE

Preparation time: 10 minutes + 10 minutes standing
Cooking time: 1 hour 50 minutes
Serves 4

2 tablespoons oil
1 large onion, sliced
2 tablespoons good-quality vindaloo curry paste
1 kg (2 lb 4 oz) chuck steak, trimmed and cubed
250 ml (9 fl oz/1 cup) beef stock
200 ml (7 fl oz) coconut cream
250 g (9 oz/1¼ cups) basmati rice
¾ teaspoon ground turmeric

1 Heat the oil in a large saucepan over medium–high heat. Add the onion and cook for 4–5 minutes, or until starting to soften. Add the curry paste and stir for 1 minute, or until fragrant. Add the steak and brown evenly for about 5 minutes.

2 Pour in the stock and bring to the boil. Reduce the heat to very low and simmer, covered, for 1 hour, or until the meat is tender. Remove the lid and cook for an extra 15 minutes to reduce the sauce.

3 Add the coconut cream, return to the boil, then simmer over low heat for a further 15–20 minutes, or until the beef is tender and the sauce has reduced.

4 About 25 minutes before the beef is ready, rinse the rice and place it in a large saucepan. Add the turmeric and 440 ml (16 fl oz/1¾ cups) water and bring to the boil. Reduce the heat to very low, then cook, covered, for 10 minutes. Remove from the heat and leave to stand, covered, for 10 minutes. Divide the rice among four wide serving bowls and top with the beef curry.

COOK'S FILE

Variation: Use chicken thighs on the bone instead of beef, if desired. Reduce the cooking time by 30 minutes and serve when the chicken is starting to fall off the bone.

LAMB KOFTA CURRY

Preparation time: 15 minutes
Cooking time: 30 minutes
Serves 4

250 g (9 oz/1¼ cups) jasmine rice
1 kg (2 lb 4 oz) lean minced (ground) lamb
1 egg, lightly beaten
2 onions, finely chopped
120 g (4¼ oz) good-quality mild Korma curry paste
4 tablespoons chopped fresh coriander (cilantro) leaves
2 garlic cloves, crushed
2 tablespoons oil
400 g (14 oz) tin diced tomatoes

1 Preheat the oven to hot 220°C (425°F/Gas 7) and lightly grease two baking trays. Bring a large saucepan of water to the boil. Add the rice and cook for 12 minutes, stirring occasionally. Drain well.

2 Meanwhile, combine the mince, egg, 1 of the onions, 2 tablespoons of the curry paste, 3 tablespoons of the coriander, 1 clove of garlic and salt. Form tablespoons of the mixture into balls and place on one of the prepared baking trays.

3 Heat 1 tablespoon of the oil in a large non-stick frying pan over medium heat. When hot, cook the balls in batches for 1 minute on each side, or until evenly golden, but not cooked through. Place on the second tray and bake for 5–7 minutes, or until cooked through.

4 Meanwhile, wipe the pan clean with paper towels. Heat the remaining oil over medium heat. Add the remaining onion and garlic and cook for 3 minutes, or until the onion is soft. Add the remaining curry paste and cook for 1 minute before adding the tomatoes and 250 ml (9 fl oz/1 cup) water. Bring to the boil, then reduce the heat to low and gently simmer for 10 minutes, or until the sauce thickens slightly. Season with salt.

5 Add the baked meatballs and their juices to the sauce, and gently stir, coating in the sauce. Simmer for 5 minutes, or until the meatballs are warmed through. Serve with rice and sprinkle with the remaining coriander.

1

2

CHICKEN SAUSAGES AND BEAN RAGOUT

Preparation time: 20 minutes
Total cooking time: 1 hour
Serves 6

6 low-fat chicken sausages (about 150 g/5½ oz each)
1 onion, chopped
4 garlic cloves, crushed
1 red capsicum (pepper), cut into 2 cm (¾ inch) pieces
½ bird's eye chilli, finely sliced
2 celery stalks, sliced
2 x 400 g (14 oz) tins chopped tomatoes
1 bay leaf
400 g (14 oz) tin borlotti beans, drained
2 small zucchini (courgettes), sliced
pinch chilli powder
1 tablespoon chopped oregano
3 tablespoons chopped basil
30 g (1 oz/½ cup) chopped parsley
1 tablespoon tomato paste (concentrated purée)
250 ml (9 fl oz/1 cup) chicken stock
1 tablespoon balsamic vinegar
1 tablespoon lemon juice

Fry the sausages in a non-stick frying pan until brown all over.

Cook the onion, garlic, capsicum, chilli and celery until soft.

1 Heat a large non-stick frying pan over medium heat. Add the sausages and cook until brown all over. Remove from the pan. Add the onion, garlic, capsicum, chilli and celery to the frying pan and cook for 5 minutes, or until soft. Add the tomato and bay leaf, then reduce the heat and simmer for 5 minutes.

2 Cut the sausages on the diagonal into 3 cm (1¼ inch) slices, then add to the tomato mixture. Cook, covered, for 5 minutes. Add the beans, zucchini, chilli powder, oregano, basil, half the parsley, tomato paste and stock. Season. Cook over low heat for another 25 minutes. Add the balsamic vinegar and simmer for 5 minutes, or until the liquid is reduced and the mixture is thick.

3 Stir in the lemon juice and the remaining parsley just before serving. Serve with crusty bread.

SPICY APRICOT CHICKEN

Preparation time: 10 minutes
Total cooking time: 20 minutes
Serves 4

750 g (1 lb 10 oz) skinless, boneless chicken thighs, cut into 5 cm (2 inch) pieces
plain (all-purpose) flour, for coating
2 tablespoons oil
2 teaspoons red curry paste
2 spring onions (scallions), sliced
415 g (15 oz) can apricot halves in light syrup
125 ml (4 fl oz/½ cup) chicken stock
200 g (7 oz) plain yoghurt
2 tablespoons chopped coriander (cilantro) leaves

1 Lightly coat the chicken in the flour. Heat the oil in a saucepan, add the curry paste and stir over low heat for 1 minute. Add the spring onion and chicken and cook, stirring, over medium heat for 2–3 minutes, or until the chicken is golden.

2 Drain the apricots and reserve 125 ml (4 fl oz/½ cup) of the juice. Add the reserved juice, apricots and chicken stock to the pan. Bring to the boil, then reduce the heat and simmer for 10 minutes, or until the chicken is tender.

3 Mix together the yoghurt and coriander and place a spoonful of the mixture over each serving of chicken. Serve with couscous or rice.

1

2

3

SICHUAN CHICKEN

Preparation time: 10 minutes
Cooking time: 25 minutes
Serves 4

¼ teaspoon five-spice powder
750 g (1 lb 10 oz) skinless, boneless chicken thighs, halved
2 tablespoons peanut oil
1 tablespoon fresh ginger, thinly sliced
1 teaspoon Sichuan peppercorns, crushed
1 teaspoon chilli bean paste (toban djan)
2 tablespoons light soy sauce
1 tablespoon Chinese rice wine
250 g (9 oz/1¼ cups) jasmine rice
600 g (1 lb 5 oz) baby bok choy (pak choy), leaves separated

1 Sprinkle five-spice powder over the chicken. Heat a wok until very hot, add half the oil and swirl to coat. Add chicken and cook for 2 minutes each side, or until browned. Remove from the wok.

2 Reduce the heat to medium and cook the ginger for 30 seconds. Add the peppercorns and chilli bean paste. Return the chicken to the wok, add soy sauce, wine and 125 ml (4 fl oz/½ cup) water, then simmer for 15–20 minutes, or until cooked.

3 Meanwhile, bring a large saucepan of water to the boil. Add rice and cook for 12 minutes. Drain well.

4 Heat the remaining oil in a saucepan. Add the bok choy and toss gently for 1 minute, or until the leaves wilt and the stems are tender. Serve with the chicken and rice.

CHILLI CON CARNE

Preparation time: 15 minutes
Cooking time: 45 minutes
Serves 4

1 tablespoon oil
1 large red onion, finely chopped
2 garlic cloves, crushed
1½ teaspoons chilli powder
1 teaspoon ground oregano
2 teaspoons ground cumin
500 g (1 lb 2 oz) lean minced (ground) beef
2 x 400 g (14 oz) tins chopped tomatoes
420 g (15 oz) tin red kidney beans, drained and rinsed
8 flour tortillas
sour cream, to serve, optional

1 Preheat the oven to 180°C (350°F/Gas 4). Heat the oil in a large saucepan, add the onion and garlic and cook, stirring, over medium heat for about 5 minutes, or until softened. Add the chilli powder, oregano and cumin and stir until fragrant. Add the mince and cook, stirring, for about 5 minutes, or until browned all over, breaking up any lumps with the back of a wooden spoon.

2 Add the tomato, beans and 125 ml (4 fl oz/½ cup) water and simmer, stirring occasionally, for about 30 minutes, or until thick. Season to taste with salt and pepper. About 10 minutes before serving, wrap the tortillas in foil and heat them in the oven, according to packet instructions, to soften. Fill the tortillas with the chilli and wrap. Serve with sour cream and, if desired, a green salad.

COOK'S FILE

Variations: Top jacket potatoes with chilli con carne and a dollop of sour cream, or serve with rice.

1

2

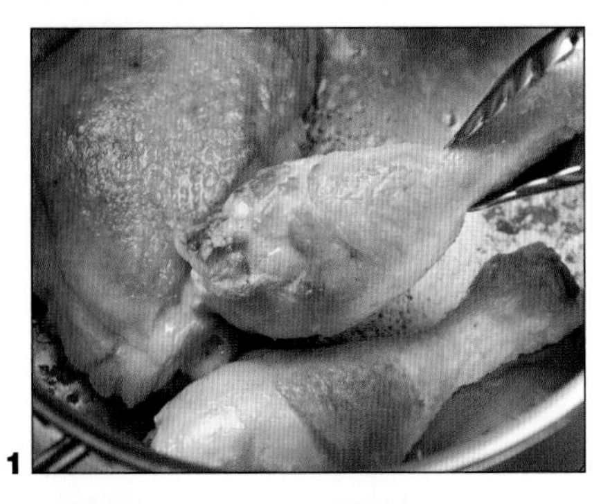

1

2

3

CHICKEN CACCIATORE WITH FETA AND BLACK OLIVES

Preparation time: 15 minutes
Total cooking time: 1 hour
Serves 4

2 tablespoons oil
8 (1.2 kg/2 lb 11 oz) chicken pieces (with skin on)
1 onion, chopped
25 g (1 oz) oregano, leaves picked
2 tablespoons tomato paste (concentrated purée)
2 x 425 g (15 oz) tins crushed tomatoes
150 g (5½ oz) black olives
150 g (5½ oz) feta cheese, crumbled

1 Heat half the oil in a saucepan and cook the chicken pieces, in batches, for 3–4 minutes, or until golden. Remove from the pan and set aside.

2 In the same saucepan, heat the remaining oil and cook the onion and half the oregano leaves for 3 minutes, or until the onion is soft. Add the tomato paste and stir for 2 minutes, then add the tomato and chicken pieces.

3 Simmer, covered, for 40–50 minutes, or until the chicken is cooked through. Add the olives and remaining oregano leaves. To serve, spoon into bowls and top with the crumbled feta.

COOK'S FILE

Serving suggestion: This dish is delicious served with fettucine.

CURRIED CHICKEN WITH ALMONDS

Preparation time: 15 minutes
Total cooking time: 1 hour 30 minutes
Serves 4–6

1 tablespoon oil
1.5 kg (3 lb 5 oz) chicken pieces, on the bone
1 onion, finely chopped
2 garlic cloves, finely chopped
2 teaspoons grated fresh ginger
2½ tablespoons curry powder (see Note)
3 x 425 g (15 oz) tins tomatoes, drained and chopped
250 ml (9 fl oz/1 cup) chicken stock
50 g (1¾ oz) slivered almonds, toasted

1 Heat the oil in a saucepan, add the chicken, in batches, and cook for 3–4 minutes each side, or until brown. Remove the chicken from the pan.

2 In the same pan, cook the onion, garlic and ginger for 2 minutes, or until soft. Add the curry powder and stir until fragrant. Add the tomato and simmer, stirring occasionally, for 10–15 minutes, or until the sauce is thick and pulpy.

3 Stir in the stock and chicken. Simmer, covered, for 30–35 minutes and then uncovered for a further 30 minutes, or until the chicken is cooked and tender. Sprinkle with the almonds and serve with steamed rice.

COOK'S FILE

Note: Curry powder is made up of a selection of ground spices, including coriander, fenugreek, cumin and mustard seeds, chilli, turmeric, ginger and cloves.

1

2

3

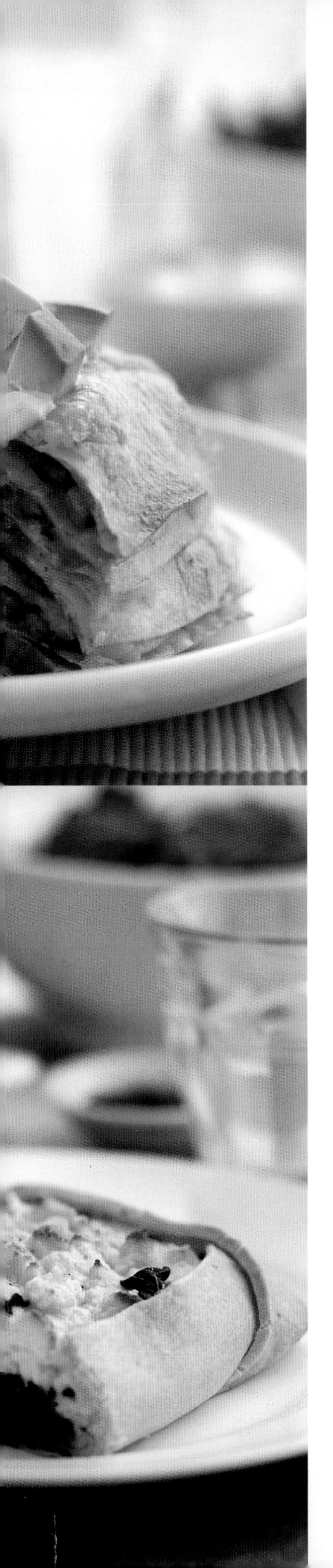

Easy bakes and roasts

ROAST LEMON CHICKEN WITH BAKED VEGETABLES

Preparation time: 15 minutes
Cooking time: 1 hour 20 minutes
Serves 4

1.5 kg (3 lb 5 oz) whole chicken
75 ml (2½ fl oz) lemon juice
½ lemon
9 cloves garlic, whole and unpeeled
4 tablespoons olive oil
1 kg (2 lb 4 oz) roasting potatoes, cut into 5 cm (2 inch) pieces
4 red onions, cut into quarters
8 small zucchini (corgettes), trimmed and cut in half lengthways
250 ml (9 fl oz/1 cup) chicken stock

1 Preheat the oven to hot 220°C (425°F/Gas 7). Wash the chicken and pat dry inside and out with paper towels, then place in a large roasting tin. Pour 25 ml (1 fl oz) of the lemon juice over the chicken, then place the lemon half and 1 clove garlic inside the chicken cavity. Brush the outside with 1 tablespoon of the oil. Season.

2 Arrange the potato and remaining garlic cloves around the chicken. Brush the potatoes with 2 tablespoons of the oil and roast for 20 minutes. Reduce the heat to moderately hot 190°C (375°F/Gas 5). Place the onion around the chicken, turning the potatoes at the same time. Return to the oven for a further 30 minutes.

3 Place the zucchini cut-side-down on a baking tray and brush with the remaining oil, then place in the oven. Baste the chicken with its pan juices and pour the remaining lemon juice over the top. Turn the onion and potatoes and roast for 20 minutes, or until the chicken is golden and the juices run clear when pierced between the breast and thigh.

4 Transfer the chicken, potatoes, garlic and onion to a serving plate, cover with foil and keep warm for 10 minutes. Check the zucchini halves are tender and nicely coloured–they may need to stay in the oven.

5 Meanwhile, to make the gravy, place the roasting tin over high heat and add the chicken stock. Stir with a wooden spoon to scrape up any sediment and boil for 7–8 minutes, or until it reduces and thickens.

6 To serve, remove the lemon and garlic from the cavity and discard. Serve the chicken with the onion, garlic, zucchini, potatoes and gravy.

1

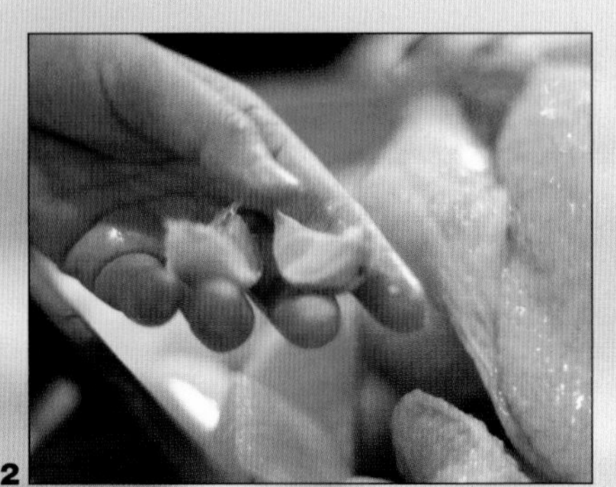
2

MUSTARD CRUSTED SCOTCH FILLET WITH ROAST VEGETABLES

Preparation time: 15 minutes + 10 minutes resting
Cooking time: 1 hour
Serves 4

16 French shallots
125 g (4½ oz/½ cup) wholegrain mustard
3 cloves garlic, crushed
1.2–1.5 kg (2 lb 10 oz–3 lb 5 oz) scotch fillet
200 g (7 oz) parsnips, cut into 2 cm (¾ inch) chunks
400 g (14 oz) potatoes, cut lengthways into wedges
200 g (7 oz) orange sweet potato, cut into wedges
4 tablespoons olive oil

1 Preheat the oven to moderately hot 200°C (400°F/Gas 6). Peel four of the French shallots, slice into thick rings and arrange them in the centre of a large roasting tin.

2 Combine the mustard and garlic, and season well with salt and pepper. Rub the mixture over the surface of the beef, then place the beef on top of the sliced shallots. Toss the parsnip, potato, sweet potato, the remaining shallots, and 3 tablespoons of the oil together, then arrange around the beef. Drizzle the remaining oil over the beef and roast for 30 minutes.

3 Season and turn the vegetables—don't worry if some of the mustard mixes through. Roast for a further 30 minutes for a medium–rare result, or until cooked to your liking. Turn the oven off, leave the door ajar and allow to rest for 10 minutes.

4 To serve, carve the beef and spoon the pan juices on the top. Serve with the roasted vegetables, whole shallots, and some steamed greens, if desired.

1

2

BALSAMIC ROASTED VEAL CUTLETS WITH RED ONION

Preparation time: 10 minutes
Cooking time: 45 minutes
Serves 4

1½ tablespoons olive oil
8 veal cutlets
4 cloves garlic, unpeeled
1 red onion, cut into thin wedges
1 tablespoon chopped fresh rosemary
250 g (9 oz) cherry tomatoes
3 tablespoons balsamic vinegar
2 teaspoons soft brown sugar
2 tablespoons chopped fresh flat-leaf (Italian) parsley

1 Preheat the oven to moderately hot 200°C (400°F/Gas 6). Heat the oil in a large frying pan over medium heat. Cook the cutlets in batches for 4 minutes on both sides, or until brown.

2 Arrange the cutlets in a single layer in a large, shallow-sided roasting tin. Add the garlic, onion, rosemary, tomatoes, vinegar and sugar. Season well with salt and freshly ground black pepper.

3 Cover tightly with foil and roast for 15 minutes. Remove the foil and roast for a further 10–15 minutes, depending on the thickness of the veal chops.

4 Transfer the cutlets, garlic, onion and tomatoes to serving plates. Stir the pan juices and spoon over the top. Garnish with the chopped parsley and serve immediately. Delicious with a creamy garlic mash and a tossed green salad.

1

AROMATIC SNAPPER PARCELS

Preparation time: 10 minutes
Cooking time: 20 minutes
Serves 4

30 g (1 oz/1 cup) loosely packed fresh basil leaves, chopped
2 large cloves garlic, chopped
1 tablespoon lemon juice
1 teaspoon grated lemon rind
3 tablespoons olive oil
4 skinless snapper fillets, trimmed and boned (about 200 g/7 oz each)
500 g (1 lb 2 oz) small new potatoes
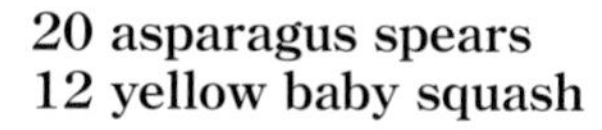
20 asparagus spears
12 yellow baby squash

1 Preheat the oven to moderately hot 200°C (400°F/Gas 6). Combine the basil, garlic, lemon juice, rind and 2 tablespoons of the olive oil. Season to taste.

2 Place a fish fillet in the centre of a sheet of foil large enough to fully enclose it. Season. Smear the fillet with 2 teaspoons of the basil mixture, then wrap into a secure parcel. Repeat with the remaining fillets. Place on a baking tray and refrigerate until required.

3 Cook the potatoes in a large saucepan of boiling water for 15–20 minutes, or until tender. Drain and keep warm. While the potatoes are cooking, brush the asparagus and squash with the remaining oil. Place on a baking tray and season with freshly ground black pepper. Bake for 8–10 minutes, or until golden and tender.

4 About 10 minutes before the vegetables are ready, place the fish parcels in the oven and cook for 5–7 minutes, or until the flesh flakes easily when tested with a fork. Check one of the parcels after 5 minutes to see if the fish is cooked through.

5 Place the opened parcels on serving plates with the vegetables, season to taste and serve.

COOK'S FILE

Variation: Use ling or tail pieces of salmon fillet instead of the snapper.

1

2

CREAMY TOMATO MEATLOAF

Preparation time: 10 minutes + refrigeration
Total cooking time: 1 hour
Serves 6

750 g (1 lb 10 oz) minced (ground) beef
170 g (6 oz/⅔ cup) sour cream
50 g (1¾ oz) tomato soup mix
1 onion, finely chopped
2 cloves garlic, crushed
3 teaspoons ground paprika
1 teaspoon chopped red chilli

1 Preheat oven to 180°C (350°F/Gas 4). Lightly grease a 21 x 14 x 7 cm (8½ x 5½ x 2¾ inch) loaf tin, line base and sides with paper. Place beef in a large bowl with remaining ingredients and mix until well combined.

2 Press mixture firmly into prepared loaf tin. Bake for 1 hour or until well browned and firm in the centre. Turn out of tin, serve sliced. Serve with salad, if desired.

COOK'S FILE

Storage time: Meatloaf may be served hot or cold. If serving hot, cook just before serving. If serving cold, meat loaf can be cooked up to 2 days before required. Store, covered, in refrigerator.

1

2

VEAL PARMIGIANA

Preparation time: 15 minutes + refrigeration
Total cooking time: 25 minutes
Serves 4

4 thin slices veal
plain (all-purpose) flour, for coating
1 egg, lightly beaten
dry breadcrumbs, for coating
30 g (1 oz) butter
3 tablespoons oil
160 g (5½ oz/½ cup) bottled chunky tomato pasta sauce
50 g (1¾ oz/½ cup) grated Parmesan cheese
75 g (2½ oz/½ cup) grated mozzarella cheese

1 Pat veal dry with paper towels. Place flour on a plate, egg in a bowl, and breadcrumbs on another plate. Coat veal with flour, dip in egg and then coat with bread crumbs, Refrigerate for approximately 1 hour.
2 Preheat oven to 180°C (350°F/ Gas 4). Brush a medium-sized ovenproof dish with oil. Heat butter and oil in a large frying pan. Add veal to pan and cook for 2–3 minutes each side or until golden. Drain on paper towels.
3 Place in a single layer in prepared dish, spoon tomato pasta sauce over and sprinkle with combined cheeses. Bake uncovered for 20–25 minutes or until golden. Serve immediately, with salad, if desired.

COOK'S FILE

Storage time: Recipe may be completed, up to baking stage, several hours ahead, covered, and refrigerated. Cook just before serving. Dish may also be frozen, without cheeses, for up to 1 month. Sprinkle cheeses on top just before cooking.
Variation: Instead of mozzarella, use Cheddar cheese.

1

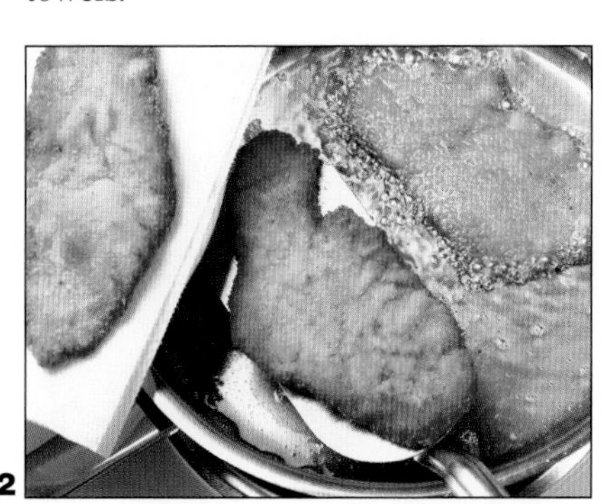
2

3

TORTILLA PIE

Preparation time: 15 minutes
Cooking time: 25 minutes
Serves 4

1 tablespoons oil
500 g (1 lb 2 oz) lean minced (ground) beef
35 g (1¼ oz) packet taco seasoning mix
420 g (15 oz) can Mexican chilli beans, drained
8 flour tortillas
250 g (9 oz/2 cups) grated Cheddar
300 g (11 oz) Mexican tomato salsa
150 g (5½ oz) sour cream
1 avocado, diced

1 Preheat the oven to moderate 180°C (350°F/Gas 4). Grease a 23 cm (9 inch) pie dish. Heat the oil in a large non-stick frying pan. Add the mince and cook for 5 minutes, or until brown, breaking up the lumps with the back of a spoon. Drain off the excess oil. Add the seasoning mix and cook for 5 minutes. Stir in the beans until heated through.

2 Lay a tortilla in the base of the pie dish, then spread 125 g (4½ oz/½ cup) of the mince mixture on top. Sprinkle with 3 tablespoons cheese and 1 tablespoon salsa. Continue layering with the remaining tortillas, mince mixture, cheese and salsa, ending with a tortilla sprinkled with a little cheese—it should end up looking like a dome shape.

3 Bake for 15 minutes, or until all the cheese has melted and browned. Cool slightly, cut into wedges and top with a dollop of sour cream and the diced avocado. Serve with a tomato salad, if desired.

1

2

MEXICAN CHICKEN BAKE

Preparation time: 15 minutes
Cooking time: 1 hour
Serves 4

165 g (5¾ oz/¾ cup) short-grain rice
300 g (10½ oz) can red kidney beans, drained and thoroughly rinsed
3½ tablespoons chopped fresh coriander (cilantro) leaves
1 tablespoon oil
600 g (1 lb 5 oz) boneless, skinless chicken thigh fillets, unrolled
2 x 200 g (7 oz) jars spicy taco sauce
250 g (9 oz/2 cups) grated Cheddar
125 g (4½ oz/½ cup) sour cream

1 Preheat the oven to moderate 180°C (350°F/Gas 4). Lightly grease a deep (7 cm/2¾ inch) round (21 cm/8¼ inch) ceramic casserole dish. Bring a large saucepan of water to the boil, add the rice and cook for 10–12 minutes, stirring occasionally. Drain.

2 In the prepared dish, combine the beans and 1½ tablespoons of the coriander, then add the rice and toss together. Lightly press the mixture so the beans are mixed into the rice and the mixture is flat.

3 Heat the oil in a large frying pan over medium–high heat. Sauté the chicken thighs for 3 minutes, then turn over. Add the spicy taco sauce, and cook for a further 3 minutes.

4 To assemble, spread half the cheese over the rice. Arrange the thighs and sauce on top in a star shape, sprinkle with 1½ tablespoons of the coriander, then sprinkle with the remaining cheese. Cover with foil.

5 Bake for 35–40 minutes, or until the mixture is bubbling and the cheese is melted and slightly browned—remove the foil for the last 5 minutes of cooking. Cut into four servings with a knife and scoop out carefully, keeping the layers intact. Serve sprinkled with the remaining coriander and a dollop of sour cream.

1

2

ROAST PEPPERED BEEF WITH ONIONS AND POTATOES

Preparation time: 15 minutes
Cooking time: 40 minutes
Serves 4

1 kg (2 lb 4 oz) piece beef sirloin
2 tablespoons freshly ground black peppercorns
1 large red onion
4 large potatoes
50 g (1¾ oz) butter
3 tablespoons beef stock
3 tablespoons red wine
500 g (1 lb 2 oz) mixed yellow and green beans

1 Preheat the oven to moderate 180°C (350°F/Gas 4). Trim the excess fat from the beef, leaving a thin layer. Press the pepper all over the beef.

2 Cut the onion and potatoes into 5 mm (¼ inch) thick slices and place in a roasting tin. Sit the beef on top, fat-side-up. Cut 40 g (1½ inch) of the butter into small pieces and dot all over the beef and potatoes. Pour in the stock and wine and bake for 35–40 minutes, for medium–rare, or until cooked to your liking. Remove the beef from the oven and rest for at least 5 minutes before carving.

3 Meanwhile, bring a saucepan of lightly salted water to the boil. Add the mixed beans and cook for 2–4 minutes, or until just tender. Drain well, then add the remaining butter and toss together. Keep warm until ready to serve.

4 To serve, divide the onion and potato mixture among four serving plates and top with slices of beef. Spoon on any pan juices and serve with the beans.

1

VEGETABLE BAKE

Preparation time: 15 minutes
Cooking time: 1 hour
Serves 4

400 g (14 oz) potatoes, thinly sliced lengthways
60 g (2¼ oz) butter, melted
1½–2 teaspoons finely chopped fresh thyme
400 g (14 oz) pumpkin, thinly sliced
300 g (10½ oz) zucchini (courgettes), thinly sliced lengthways
250 ml (9 fl oz/1 cup) Italian tomato passata
50 g (1¾ oz/½ cup) grated Parmesan

1 Preheat the oven to warm 170°C (325°F/Gas 3). Grease a 1.5 litre (6 cup) rectangular ovenproof dish. Combine the potato with one third each of the butter and thyme. Season, then place in the base of the prepared dish.

2 Combine the pumpkin and another third of the butter and thyme. Season and press onto the potato. Combine the zucchini with the remaining butter and thyme. Season and press on to the pumpkin.

3 Spread the passata evenly over the top and cover with a piece of greased foil. Bake for 45 minutes, remove the foil and sprinkle with the grated Parmesan. Bake for a further 15 minutes, or until the top is golden brown and the vegetables are cooked through. Serve with a salad and crusty bread, if desired.

1

2

ROASTED MARYLANDS WITH SAGE AND PROSCIUTTO

Preparation time: 10 minutes + marinating
Total cooking time: 40 minutes
Serves 4

2 tablespoons oil
2 teaspoons seeded mustard
1 clove garlic, crushed
4 pieces chicken Maryland (leg quarter)
16 sage leaves
4 slices prosciutto

1 Combine oil, mustard, garlic and pepper in a small bowl. Using a sharp knife, make diagonal cuts across the top of each chicken maryland. Place chicken in a nonmetal dish. Brush oil mixture over chicken. Cover and refrigerate for several hours or overnight.

2 Preheat oven to 180°C (350°F/ Gas 4). Transfer chicken to large baking dish. Lay sage leaves over chicken Marylands. Cut prosciutto slices cross-ways in half, lay over the sage. Bake 40 minutes or until golden and tender.

1

2

COOK'S FILE

Hint: Delicious served with steamed carrots and beans or broccoli.

ROAST CHICKEN WITH FRESH HERB STUFFING

Preparation time: 20 minutes + 10 minutes standing
Total cooking time: 1 hour 30 minutes
Serves 4–6

3 slices wholegrain bread, crusts removed
3 spring onions (scallions), chopped
60 g (2¼ oz/1 cup) chopped parsley
1 tablespoon chopped thyme
1 tablespoon chopped oregano
1 teaspoon grated lemon zest
1 egg, lightly beaten
1.4 kg (3 lb 4 oz) chicken
1 tablespoon oil

1 Preheat oven to 180°C (350°F/Gas 4). Cut bread into small squares; place in a medium bowl. Add onion, herbs, lemon zest and egg. Mix well.

2 Remove giblets and excess fat from chicken. Wipe and pat dry chicken with paper towels. Spoon stuffing into chicken cavity; close cavity with a toothpick or skewer. Tie legs together with string. Place on roasting rack in a deep baking dish, brush with oil. Roast the chicken for 1 hour 25 minutes or until brown and tender. Remove from oven and leave, loosely covered with foil, in a warm place; for 10 minutes. Remove toothpick, and string before carving. Garnish with sprigs of fresh herbs and slices of lemon, if desired.

1

2

RACK OF PORK WITH FIG AND MARSALA SAUCE

Preparation time: 10 minutes + 30 minutes soaking
Cooking time: 1 hour 40 minutes
Serves 4

300 g (10½ oz) dessert figs, quartered
4 tablespoons Marsala
2 teaspoons Dijon mustard
125 ml (4 fl oz/½ cup) chicken stock
1.5 kg (3 lb 5 oz) rack of pork, tied
120 ml (4 fl oz) oil
1 large red onion, sliced
18 fresh sage leaves
300 g (10½ oz/cup) beans, trimmed

1 Preheat the oven to very hot 240°C (475°F/Gas 9). Soak the figs, Marsala, mustard and stock for 30 minutes.

2 Score the rind of the pork in lines spaced 5 cm (2 inches) apart, brush with 2 tablespoons of the oil and season. Place in a large roasting tin, cook for 15 minutes, then reduce the heat to moderately hot 200°C (400°F/Gas 6). Add the onion, cook for 40 minutes, then add the fig mixture, cooking for 30–40 minutes, or until the pork juices run clear when the thickest section is pierced with a skewer.

3 Meanwhile, heat the remaining oil in a small saucepan over high heat. Add the sage leaves a few at a time for 30 seconds per batch. Remove with a slotted spoon and drain.

4 Remove the pork and onion pieces from the oven and allow the meat to rest for 5 minutes. Drain the excess fat from the roasting tin. Reduce the sauce on the stovetop for 5 minutes, stirring to scrape up any sediment stuck to the base of the pan.

5 Bring a saucepan of water to the boil, add the beans and cook for 4 minutes. Drain, season. Keep warm.

6 Slice the pork into portions, pour on the sauce and garnish with the sage leaves. Serve with the onions, beans and, if desired, mashed potato.

1

2

TUNA AND VEGETABLE BAKE

Preparation time: 15 minutes
Total cooking time: 35 minutes
Serves 4

2 tablespoons oil
1 onion, chopped
1 red capsicum (pepper), chopped
2 zucchini (courgettes), chopped
425 g (15 oz) can tomatoes
425 g (15 oz) can tuna, drained and flaked
2 potatoes, coarsely grated
125 g (4½ oz/1 cup) grated Cheddar cheese

1

2

1 Preheat oven to 210°C (415°F/ Gas 6–7). Heat oil in pan; add onion, capsicum and zucchini. Stir over high heat for 3 minutes or until tender.

2 Add undrained, crushed tomato reduce heat to low, simmer 3 minutes. Stir in drained, flaked tuna. Spread over base of a 1.5-litre (6 cup) ovenproof dish. Squeeze liquid from potato. Combine potato and cheese, spread over tuna mixture. Bake 25 minutes. Cook under hot grill (broiler) until crisp and golden brown.

COOK'S FILE

Hint: Use pontiac or old potatoes for this recipe

BLUE EYE COD CUTLETS IN A SPICY TOMATO SAUCE

Preparation time: 5 minutes
Cooking time: 25 minutes
Serves 4

4 blue eye cod cutlets, 2.5 cm (1 inch) thick (about 250 g 9 oz each)
250 g (9 oz/1¼ cups) long-grain rice
2 tablespoons oil
1 teaspoon coriander seeds, lightly crushed
1 teaspoon black mustard seeds
1½ tablespoons sambal oelek
400 g (14 oz) can diced tomatoes
1 teaspoon garam masala
300 g (10½ oz) baby English spinach leaves

1 Preheat the oven to moderate 180°C (350°F/Gas 4). Pat the cutlets dry with paper towels.

2 Bring a large saucepan of water to the boil. Add the rice and cook for 12 minutes, stirring occasionally. Drain well.

3 Meanwhile, heat 1 tablespoon of the oil in a saucepan over medium heat. When hot, add the coriander and mustard seeds–the mustard seeds should start to pop after about 30 seconds. Add the sambal oelek and cook for 30 seconds, then stir in the tomatoes and the garam masala. Bring to the boil, then reduce the heat to low and simmer, covered, for 6–8 minutes, or until the sauce thickens.

4 Heat the remaining oil in a large non-stick frying pan over medium heat. Add the cutlets and cook for 1 minute each side, or until evenly browned but not cooked through. Transfer to a 28 cm x 18.5 cm (11¼ inch x 7 inch) ceramic baking dish. Spoon the tomato sauce over the cutlets and bake for 10 minutes, or until the fish is cooked through.

5 Meanwhile, wash the spinach and put in a saucepan with just the water clinging to the leaves. Cook, covered, for 1 minute, or until the spinach has wilted. Serve the fish cutlets topped with sauce, with the spinach and some steamed rice.

1

2

1

2

SAUSAGE AND BEAN HOT POT WITH ROASTED ORANGE SWEET POTATO

Preparation time: 15 minutes
Cooking time: 50 minutes
Serves 4

1 kg (2 lb 4 oz) spicy Italian-style sausages
2 cloves garlic, roughly chopped
2 x 400 g (14 oz) cans cannellini beans
2 x 425 g (15 oz) cans crushed tomatoes
2 teaspoons Dijon mustard
750 g (1 lb 10 oz) orange sweet potato, cut into 3 cm (1¼ inch) cubes
2 tablespoons olive oil
2 tablespoons coarsely chopped fresh parsley

1 Preheat the oven to moderately hot 200°C (400°F/Gas 6). Cook the sausages in a large frying pan over medium heat for 8–10 minutes, or until golden. Cut into 5 cm pieces and place in a 4 litre (16 cup) casserole dish. Add the garlic, beans, tomato, mustard and 2 tablespoons water to the dish and season with pepper. Stir well and cover with a lid. Place in the oven.

2 Meanwhile, toss the sweet potato with the oil and place snugly in a baking dish. Sprinkle with salt. Place in the oven with the casserole dish and bake for 25 minutes. Uncover the casserole dish and bake for a further 10–15 minutes, or until the hot pot is golden and bubbling and the sweet potato is soft and lightly golden brown. Serve the hot pot garnished with the parsley and the sweet potato on the side.

COOK'S FILE

Hint: Make the hot pot up to 24 hours in advance and reheat to serve. You may need to add 125 ml (4 fl oz/½ cup) water as it tends to thicken when refrigerated.

CHICKEN AND ARTICHOKE PIZZA

Preparation time: 15 minutes
Total cooking time: 25 minutes
Serves 4

2 tablespoons extra virgin olive oil
170 g (6 oz) jar marinated artichokes, drained, quartered and juice reserved
2 large chicken thigh fillets, cut into bite-sized pieces
1 ready-made tomato pizza base (26 cm/10½ inch diameter)
1 small red onion, finely sliced
½ red capsicum (pepper), sliced
12 Kalamata olives
200 g (7 oz) bocconcini cheese, sliced

1 Preheat the oven to 220°C (425°F/Gas 7). Heat the oil in a frying pan, add 2 tablespoons reserved artichoke juice and the chicken and cook over high heat for 3–4 minutes, or until the chicken is cooked through.
2 Place the pizza base on an oven tray and scatter the chicken evenly over the base, reserving the oil from cooking. Scatter the artichokes, onion, capsicum and olives over the chicken, season with salt and black pepper, and add the bocconcini slices. Spoon the oil from cooking over the topping.
3 Bake on the top shelf of the oven for 15–20 minutes, or until the topping begins to brown. Cut into wedges and serve.

COOK'S FILE

Variation: For a more cheesy base, sprinkle with grated mozzarella before assembling the pizza topping.

1

2

3

OVEN 'FRIED' CHICKEN

Preparation time: 15 minutes
Total cooking time: 50 minutes
Serves 4–6

1.5 kg (3 lb 5 oz) chicken drumsticks
185 ml (6 fl oz/¾ cup) buttermilk
1½ tablespoons olive oil
150 g (5½ oz/1 cup) polenta (cornmeal)
100 g (3½ oz/1 cup) dry breadcrumbs
½ teaspoon chilli powder
2 eggs
40 g (1½ oz) unsalted butter, melted

1 Preheat the oven to 180°C (350°F/Gas 4). Grease a foil-lined baking tray. Place the drumsticks in a bowl, add the buttermilk and oil and toss to coat.

2 In a separate bowl, combine the polenta, breadcrumbs and chilli powder, and season to taste with salt and freshly ground black pepper. Put the eggs in a small bowl and whisk with 1 tablespoon water.

3 Dip the chicken in the egg mixture, then coat with the polenta mixture, pressing with your fingers to make the crumbs stick. Arrange on the baking tray and drizzle with melted butter. Bake for 45–50 minutes, or until the chicken is crisp and golden. Serve with sweet potato mash and a green salad.

COOK'S FILEP

Note: Oven-frying delivers a crisp, crunchy crust with a lot less fat than traditional deep-frying. For an even leaner version, remove the skin from the chicken before coating. To make the 'fried' chicken really moist, marinate the drumsticks in the buttermilk and oil for up to 8 hours.

1

2

3

THAI GINGER FISH WITH CORIANDER BUTTER

Preparation time: 15 minutes
Cooking time: 10 minutes
Serves 4

60 g (2¼ oz) butter, at room temperature
1 tablespoon finely chopped fresh coriander (cilantro) leaves
2 tablespoons lime juice
1 tablespoon oil
1 tablespoon grated palm sugar (jaggery)
4 fresh long red chillies, seeded and chopped
2 stems lemon grass, trimmed
4 firm white fish fillets (blue eye cod or John Dory) (about 200 g/7 oz each)
1 lime, thinly sliced
1 tablespoon finely shredded fresh ginger

1 Thoroughly mix the butter and coriander and roll it into a log. Wrap the log in plastic wrap and chill in the refrigerator until required.

2 Preheat the oven to moderately hot 200°C (400°F/Gas 6). Combine the lime juice, oil, palm sugar and chilli in a small non-metallic bowl and stir until the sugar has dissolved. Cut the lemon grass into halves.

3 Place a piece of lemon grass in the centre of a sheet of foil large enough to fully enclose one fillet. Place a fish fillet on top and smear the surface with the lime juice mixture. Top with some lime slices and ginger shreds, then wrap into a secure parcel. Repeat with the remaining ingredients to make four parcels.

4 Place the parcels in an ovenproof dish and bake for 8–10 minutes, or until the fish flakes easily when tested with a fork.

5 To serve, place the parcels on individual serving plates and serve open with slices of coriander butter, steamed rice and steamed greens.

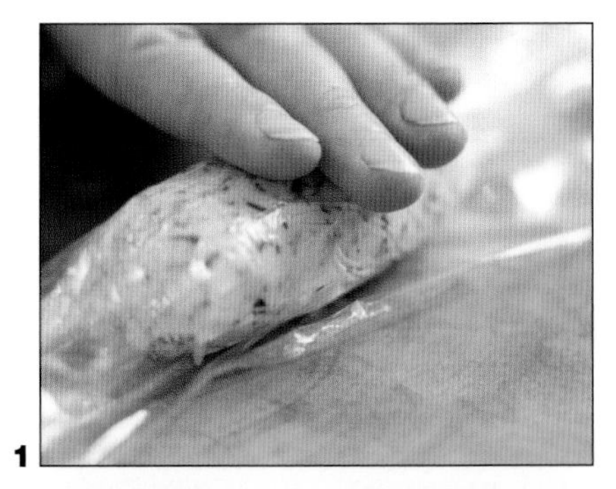

1

2

3

MOROCCAN ROAST LAMB WITH MINT COUSCOUS

Preparation time: 10 minutes + 10 minutes resting
Cooking time: 1 hour 15 minutes
Serves 4

2 tablespoons olive oil
3 teaspoons ground cumin
3 teaspoons ground coriander
3 teaspoons sweet paprika
3 cloves garlic, crushed
1.5 kg (3 lb 5 oz) easy-carve leg of lamb
245 g (9 oz/1⅓ cups) couscous
2 tablespoons chopped fresh mint

1 Preheat the oven to moderate 180°C (350°F/Gas 4). Combine the oil, spices and 2 cloves crushed garlic to form a smooth paste. Season with salt and pepper. Rub a thick coating of the paste all over the lamb. Place on a rack in a roasting tin and roast for 1 hour 15 minutes, basting two or three times. Turn off the heat, leave the oven door ajar and allow to rest for 10 minutes.

2 Meanwhile, place the couscous in a heatproof bowl with 500 ml (17 fl oz/2 cups) boiling water. Stir in the mint, the remaining garlic and ½ teaspoon salt. Cover and leave for 5 minutes, or until all the water has been absorbed, then gently fluff with a fork.

3 To serve, carve the lamb into thick slices and place on a bed of couscous. Pour the pan juices into a small jug and serve with the lamb. Garnish with fresh mint leaves, if desired.

COOK'S FILE

Note: If roasted for 1 hour 15 minutes the lamb will be medium–well done. This gives good flavour right through the meat, while basting keeps it succulent.

1

INDIVIDUAL BEEF WELLINGTONS

Preparation time: 20 minutes + refrigeration
Total cooking time: 15 minutes
Serves 4

4 beef eye fillet steaks, approximately 4 cm (1½ inches) thick
20 g (¾ oz) butter
1 tablespoon oil
100 g (3½ oz) pâté
100 g (3½ oz) button mushrooms, finely sliced
4 sheets puff pastry
1 egg yolk

1 Tie string around steaks to keep round shape. Heat butter and oil in heavy-based frying pan. Add steaks and cook over high heat 2 minutes. Turn; cook for another 2 minutes or until done to your liking. Remove from heat; cover and allow to cool.

2 Remove string from steaks. Spread a layer of pate on one side of each steak. Press mushrooms on pâté. Place steak, mushroom-side down on sheet of pastry. Trim and fit pastry to form a neat parcel with folds on the underside. Seal with combined egg yolk and 2 teaspoons water.

Use pastry scraps to decorate top of the parcel. Make 2 slits on top of pastry. Brush with egg mixture. Repeat with remaining steaks. Refrigerate parcels for about 1 hour. Preheat oven to 210°C (415°F/Gas 6–7). Bake for 5 minutes. Reduce heat to 180°C (350°F/Gas 4) and bake for another 8–10 minutes or until pastry is cooked. Serve with baked or steamed vegetables of your choice.

1

2

LEMON GARLIC CHICKEN

Preparation time: 5 minutes + marinating
Total cooking time: 1 hour
Serves 4

4 pieces chicken Maryland (leg quarter)
4 tablespoons lemon juice
4 cloves garlic, crushed
60 g (2¼ oz) butter, melted
1 teaspoon ground paprika

1 Place chicken pieces in a non-metal dish. Combine lemon juice, garlic, butter, paprika and pepper. Pour mixture over chicken. Cover and refrigerate for several hours or overnight.

2 Preheat oven to 180°C (350°F/Gas 4). Transfer chicken to a baking dish. Bake, brushing occasionally with lemon mixture, for 1 hour or until chicken is tender and golden brown. Garnish with lemon wedges, if desired.

COOK'S FILE

Hint: Bottled lemon juice is available from supermarkets and delicatessens.
Variations: Other chicken pieces such as breasts or thighs may be used.

LEEK AND ASPARAGUS FRITTATA

Preparation time: 10 minutes
Total cooking time: 35 minutes
Serves 4

30 g (1 oz) butter
1 leek, finely sliced
340 g (12 oz) can asparagus cuts, drained
2 tablespoons chopped sundried tomatoes
5 eggs
125 ml (4 fl oz/½ cup) cream

1 Preheat oven to 180°C (350°F/Gas 4). Grease a 23 cm (9 inch) pie plate or flan dish. Melt butter in pan and add sliced leek. Stir over medium heat for 2 minutes or until softened. Drain on paper towels.

2 Combine leek, asparagus and sundried tomatoes in a bowl. Spread evenly into prepared dish. Whisk eggs, cream, salt and pepper together and pour over vegetables. Bake for 30 minutes or until golden brown.

COOK'S FILE

Note: Sundried tomatoes are available from supermarkets and delicatessens.

TUNA MORNAY

Preparation time: 25 minutes
Total cooking time: 20-25 minutes
Serves 4–6

425 g (15 oz) can tuna in oil, drained
1 tablespoon lemon juice
30 g (1 oz) butter
1 red onion, diced
2 sticks celery, chopped
440 g (15½ oz) can cream of asparagus soup
4 tablespoons milk
80 g (2¾ oz/1 cup) fresh breadcrumbs
125 g (4½ oz/½ cup) grated Cheddar cheese
1 tablespoon chopped parsley

1 Preheat oven to 180°C (350°F/ Gas 4). Grease a 1-litre (4 cup) oven proof dish. Combine tuna, lemon juice and freshly ground black pepper in a bowl. Spread evenly over base of prepared dish.

2 Heat a frying pan over medium heat. Melt butter, add onion. Stir for 5 minutes or until onion softens. Add celery. Pour in soup and stir until combined. Add milk. When mixture is simmering, remove from heat and pour over the tuna. Sprinkle combined breadcrumbs, cheese and parsley over the top. Bake, uncovered, for 15 minutes or until the cheese has melted and top is golden. Serve hot.

COOK'S FILE

Variations: Substitute 500 g (1 lb 2 oz) boned white fish fillets for tuna.

1

2

ARTICHOKE, OLIVE AND GOAT'S CHEESE PIZZA

Preparation time: 10 minutes
Cooking time: 20 minutes
Serves 4

25 cm (10 inch) purchased pizza base
4 tablespoons Italian tomato passata
150 g (5½ oz) marinated artichokes, quartered
70 g (2½ oz) pitted Kalamata olives
1 clove garlic, thinly sliced
50 g (1¾ oz) goat's cheese, crumbled
good-quality olive oil, to drizzle
2 tablespoons chopped fresh oregano

1 Preheat the oven to hot 220°C (425°F/Gas 7). Place the pizza base on a baking tray, then spread with the tomato passata. Evenly scatter the artichoke pieces, olives and the garlic over the passata, then top with the crumbled goat's cheese.
2 Lightly drizzle the surface of the pizza with olive oil and bake for 20 minutes, or until golden. Sprinkle with fresh oregano and season with salt and freshly ground black pepper. Cut into wedges and serve.

1

SHEPHERD'S PIE WITH GARLIC MASH

Preparation time: 15 minutes
Cooking time: 1 hour 40 minutes
Serves 4

1½ tablespoons oil
1 large onion, finely chopped
1 carrot, finely diced
8 garlic cloves, peeled
750 g (1 lb 10 oz) lean minced (grand) lamb
375 ml (13 fl oz/1½ cups) Italian tomato passata
300 ml (10½ fl oz) beef stock
800 g (1 lb 12 oz) potatoes, cut into large chunks
30 g (1 oz) butter

1 Heat the oil in a large saucepan over medium heat. Add the onion and carrot, and cook for 5 minutes, or until softened. Crush 2 garlic cloves and sauté with the onion mixture for another minute. Add the lamb mince and stir well, breaking up any lumps with the back of a wooden spoon. Cook for 5 minutes, or until browned and cooked through. Drain off any excess fat with a large spoon, then add the tomato passata and 250 ml (9 fl oz/1 cup) of the stock. Cover and bring to the boil. Reduce the heat to medium–low and simmer for 25 minutes. Uncover and cook for a further 20 minutes, or until the sauce reduces and thickens. Preheat the oven to moderately hot 200°C (400°F/Gas 6).

2 Meanwhile, place the potato in a saucepan of boiling water with the remaining garlic and cook for 15–20 minutes, or until tender. Drain well, then return to the pan over low heat, stirring to evaporate any excess water. Remove the pan from the heat, add the butter and the remaining stock and mash until smooth. Season.

3 Transfer the lamb mixture to a 1.5 litre (6 cup) ovenproof ceramic dish. Spoon the mashed potato over the top and spread it out evenly. Use a fork to swirl the surface. Bake for 40 minutes, or until the potato is golden brown.

COOK'S FILE

Ahead of time: The lamb mixture can be made the day before and refrigerated or in advance and frozen until required.

1

2

SWISS ONION TART

Preparation time: 15 minutes
Total cooking time: 55 minutes
Serves 4

2 sheets frozen shortcrust pastry, thawed
2 tablespoons oil
3 medium onions, sliced
125 g (4½ oz/½ cup) sour cream
2 eggs
65 g (2¼ oz/½ cup) finely grated Gruyère cheese
cayenne pepper

1 Preheat oven to 210°C (415°F/Gas 6–7). Fit pastry into a 20 cm (8 inch) fluted flan tin; trim edges. Cut a sheet of greaseproof paper large enough to cover pastry-lined tin. Spread a layer of dried beans or rice evenly over paper. Bake for 10 minutes, remove from oven. Discard paper and beans or rice. Return pastry to oven for 5 minutes or until lightly golden. Reduce oven to 180°C (350°F/Gas 4).

2 Heat oil in pan and add onion. Cook over low heat, stirring often, for 15 minutes or until lightly browned and very tender. Spread over pastry.

3 Whisk sour cream and eggs in bowl until smooth; add cheese; stir until combined. Place flan tin on baking tray. Pour egg mixture over onion and sprinkle lightly with cayenne. Bake 40 minutes or until filling is set. May be garnished with fresh herbs.

COOK'S FILE

Storage time: Onion can be cooked and filling prepared several hours ahead. Store, covered, in refrigerator. Assemble tart and bake just before serving.

1

2

3

CAULIFLOWER WITH TOMATO SAUCE

Preparation time: 20 minutes
Total cooking time: 20–25 minutes
Serves 4

800 g (1 lb 12 oz) cauliflower
2–3 tablespoons olive oil
80 g (2¾ oz/1 cup) coarse fresh white breadcrumbs
500 g (1 lb 2 oz/2 cups) bottled tomato pasta sauce
2 tablespoons shredded basil leaves
50 g (1¾ oz/½ cup) grated Parmesan cheese
60 g (2¼ oz/½ cup) grated Cheddar cheese

1 Preheat oven to 180°C (350°F/ Gas 4). Trim cauliflower into small florets. Brush a deep ovenproof dish with melted butter or oil. Place florets in dish. Heat oil in a frying pan; add the fresh breadcrumbs and toss over medium heat until crisp and golden. Season with salt and pepper. Remove from pan and drain on paper towels.

2 Combine tomato pasta sauce and basil. Pour over cauliflower in prepared dish. Sprinkle with combined breadcrumbs and cheeses. Sprinkle with extra pepper. Bake for 20–25 minutes or until cauliflower is tender, cheese has melted and top is brown.

COOK'S FILE

Note: Choose a chunky tomato pasta sauce for this dish.

1

2

BAKED MEDITERRANEAN PORK CUTLETS

Preparation time: 15 minutes + 20 minutes marinating
Cooking time: 45 minutes
Serves 4

4 large pork loin cutlets, trimmed
2 tablespoons olive oil
2 cloves garlic, finely chopped
1 tablespoon finely chopped fresh rosemary
2 tablespoons fresh thyme
2 tablespoons balsamic vinegar
4 Roma (plum) tomatoes, halved lengthways
1 large red capsicum (pepper)
4 small zucchini (courgettes), trimmed and halved lengthways

1 Preheat the oven to hot 220°C (425°F/Gas 7) and lightly grease a baking tin. Arrange the pork cutlets in a single layer in the tin. Combine the olive oil, garlic, rosemary, thyme and 1 tablespoon of the balsamic vinegar, then spoon half the mixture over the pork cutlets. Season to taste with salt and black pepper. Cover with plastic wrap and marinate for 20 minutes.
2 Place 2 tomato halves, cut-side-down, on each cutlet and sprinkle the tomatoes with the remaining balsamic vinegar.
3 Remove the seeds from the capsicum and cut into 2 cm (¾ inch) strips. Toss the capsicum and zucchini with the remaining herb mixture, then add to the dish around the cutlets. Bake for 45 minutes, or until cooked through and well browned. Season to taste. Serve the cutlets with the roast vegetables, a green salad and crusty bread.

1

RUSTIC GREEK PIE

Preparation time: 15 minutes
Cooking time: 30 minutes
Serves 4

450 g (1 lb) packet frozen spinach, thawed
1 large sheet ready-rolled shortcrust pastry, thawed
3 cloves garlic, finely chopped
150 g (5½ oz) haloumi, grated
120 g feta (4¼ oz), crumbled
1 tablespoon fresh oregano sprigs
2 eggs
3 tablespoons cream
lemon wedges, to serve

1 Preheat the oven to moderately hot 200°C (400°F/Gas 6). Squeeze the excess liquid from the spinach.
2 Place the pastry on a baking tray and spread the spinach in the middle, leaving a 3 cm (1¼ inch) border around the edge. Sprinkle the garlic over the spinach and pile the haloumi and feta on top. Sprinkle with oregano and season well. Cut a short slit into each corner of the pastry, then tuck each side of pastry over to form a border around the filling.
3 Lightly beat the eggs with the cream and carefully pour the egg mixture over the spinach filling. Bake for 25–30 minutes, or until the pastry is golden and the filling is set. Serve with the lemon wedges and a fresh green salad.

1

2

BEEF AND VEGETABLE BAKE

Preparation time: 35 minutes
Total cooking time: 40 minutes
Serves 4

30 g (1 oz) butter
750 g (1 lb 10 oz) potatoes, peeled, very thinly sliced
2 small leeks, sliced or 2 onions, thinly sliced
20 g (¾ oz) butter, extra
1 red capsicum (pepper), sliced
1 tablespoon oil
750 g (1 lb 10 oz) lean minced (ground) beef
250 ml (9 fl oz/1 cup) puréed tomato
4 tablespoons cream
grated Cheddar cheese, optional

1 Preheat oven to 180°C (350°F/Gas 4). Melt butter in a large pan and add potato. Cook over medium–high heat, turning occasionally, for 5 minutes or until tender. Remove from pan. Add leek or onion to pan and stir for 3–5 minutes or until soft. Remove from pan. Add extra butter and capsicum; cook for 3–5 minutes or until softened; remove from pan.
2 Heat oil in pan; add beef. Cook over high heat for 5–10 minutes or until meat is well browned and all the liquid has evaporated. Use a fork to break up any lumps of beef as it cooks. Add puréed tomato and cream to pan; season with salt and pepper. Stir until combined.
3 Transfer mince mixture to 1.5-litre (6 cup) ovenproof dish. Top with combined potato, leek and capsicum. Sprinkle with cheese, if desired. Bake for 30 minutes or until potato is brown.

COOK'S FILE

Storage time: This dish can be made a day in advance. Store, covered with plastic wrap, in refrigerator.

1

2

3

GLAZED HONEY PORK RIBS

Preparation time: 10 minutes + marinating
Total cooking time: 45 minutes
Serves 4

4 tablespoons honey
4 tablespoons plum sauce
4 tablespoons cold, strong tea
2 tablespoons soy sauce
1 tablespoon grated fresh ginger
2 cloves garlic, crushed
½ teaspoon Chinese five-spice powder
1.5 kg (3 lb 5 oz) pork ribs

1 Place all ingredients, except pork ribs, in a jug. Stir well to combine. Place pork in a shallow non-metallic dish and pour on marinade. Brush to coat thoroughly. Cover and refrigerate overnight or several hours.

2 Preheat oven to 180°C (350°F/ Gas 4). Drain pork, reserve marinade. Place pork on a rack in a large baking dish. Bake for 45 minutes or until tender and golden. Turn pork occasionally and brush with reserved marinade during cooking. Garnish with shredded spring onion (scallions).

COOK'S FILE

Storage time: Pork can be marinated a day in advance. Store, covered, in refrigerator. Cook just before serving.

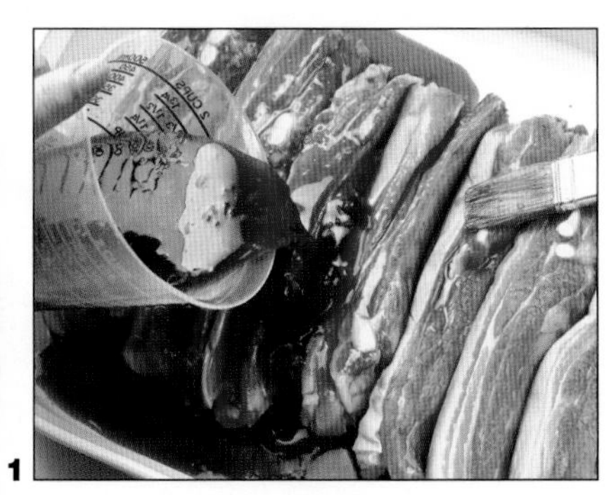

1

2

MUSHROOM POT PIES

Preparation time: 15 minutes
Cooking time: 55 minutes
Serves 4

100 ml (3½ fl oz) olive oil
1 leek, sliced
1 clove garlic, crushed
1 kg (2 lb 4 oz) large field mushrooms, roughly chopped
1 teaspoon chopped fresh thyme
300 ml (10½ fl oz) cream
1 sheet ready-rolled puff pastry, thawed
1 egg yolk, beaten, to glaze

1 Preheat the oven to moderate 180°C (350°F/Gas 4). Heat 1 tablespoon of the oil in a frying pan over medium heat. Cook the leek and garlic for 5 minutes, or until the leek is soft and translucent. Transfer to a large saucepan.

2 Heat the remaining oil in the frying pan over high heat and cook the mushrooms in two batches, stirring frequently, for 5–7 minutes per batch, or until the mushrooms have released their juices, are soft and slightly coloured. Transfer to the saucepan, then add the thyme.

3 Place the saucepan over high heat and stir in the cream until well mixed. Cook, stirring occasionally, for 7–8 minutes, or until the cream has reduced to a thick sauce. Remove from the heat and season well.

4 Divide the filling among four 315 ml (10¾ fl oz/1¼ cup) ramekins or ovenproof bowls. Cut the pastry into rounds slightly larger than each dish. Brush the rim of the ramekins with a little of the egg yolk, place the pastry on top and press down to seal. Brush the top with the remaining egg yolk. Place the ramekins on a metal tray. Bake for 20–25 minutes, or until the pastry has risen and is golden brown. Great with mashed potato and a salad.

COOK'S FILE

Variation: To make 1 large pie, transfer the filling to a 20 cm (8 inch) ceramic pie dish or 1.5 litre (6 cup) ovenproof dish. Brush the rim with a little egg yolk, place the pastry on top and press down to seal. Trim the pastry and decorate the centre with pastry shapes, if desired. Brush with the remaining egg yolk and bake for 30–35 minutes, or until golden brown.

1

2

3

RACK OF LAMB WITH MUSTARD CRUST AND PARSLEY POTATOES

Preparation time: 15 minutes
Cooking time: 45 minutes
Serves 4

2 racks of lamb (6 chops per rack), trimmed
3 tablespoons oil
160 g (5½ oz/2 cups) fresh breadcrumbs
3 cloves garlic, chopped
1 teaspoon grated lemon rind
10 g (¼ oz/½ cup) fresh flat-leaf (Italian) parsley, finely chopped
2 tablespoons tarragon Dijon mustard
150 g (5½ oz) unsalted butter, softened
400 g (14 oz) baby new potatoes

1 Preheat the oven to hot 220°C (425°F/Gas 7). Score the fat side of the racks in a criss-cross pattern. Rub 1 tablespoon of the oil over the racks and season well. Heat the remaining oil in a frying pan over medium heat and cook the racks for 5–8 minutes, or until the surface is completely brown. Remove from the pan.

2 Combine the breadcrumbs, garlic, lemon rind and three quarters of the parsley. Add the mustard and 100 g (3½ oz) of the butter to form a paste. Firmly press a layer of breadcrumb mixture over the fat side of the racks, then place in a roasting tin. Bake for 25 minutes, or until the breadcrumbs appear brown and crisp and the meat is cooked to medium. For well-done, continue to bake for 10 minutes, or until cooked to your liking. Cover the breadcrumb crust with foil to prevent it burning, if necessary.

3 About 25 minutes before the lamb is ready, toss the potatoes with the remaining butter until well coated. Season, then put in a roasting tin. Bake for 20 minutes, or until brown, then remove, sprinkle with the remaining parsley and season. To serve, cut the racks in half using the bones as a guide. Serve with the pan juices, potatoes and a tossed salad.

1

CHICKEN AND LEEK PIES

Preparation time: 15 minutes + cooling
Cooking time: 1 hour
Serves 4

875 ml (30 fl oz/3½ cup) chicken and herb stock
4 chicken breasts (about 200 g/7 oz each)
60 g (2¼ oz) butter
1 leek, thinly sliced
50 g (1¾ oz) plain (all-purpose) flour
300 ml (10½ fl oz) cream
155 g (5½ oz/1 cup) fresh or frozen peas, blanched
1 sheet ready-rolled puff pastry, thawed

Place the stock in a deep-sided frying pan then bring to the boil. Reduce the heat to medium–low so the liquid is just simmering, then gently poach the chicken for 10–12 minutes, or until just cooked (add 100 ml/3½ fl oz water if needed to keep the chicken covered). Allow to cool in the liquid. Remove the chicken, reserving the liquid, and cut into bite-sized pieces.

1 Melt the butter in a saucepan over medium heat and cook the leek for 5 minutes, or until soft. Add the flour and cook, stirring, until it starts to bubble. Stir in 250 ml (9 fl oz/1 cup) of the reserved liquid and cook until it 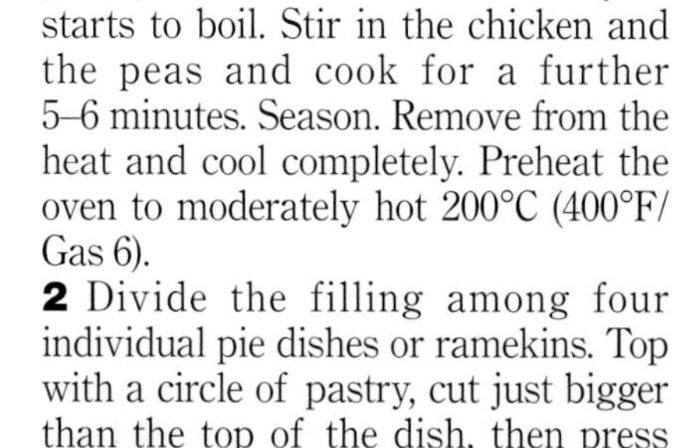starts to thicken. Add the cream, reserving 1 tablespoon to glaze the pastry. Cook until the mixture just starts to boil. Stir in the chicken and the peas and cook for a further 5–6 minutes. Season. Remove from the heat and cool completely. Preheat the oven to moderately hot 200°C (400°F/Gas 6).

2 Divide the filling among four individual pie dishes or ramekins. Top with a circle of pastry, cut just bigger than the top of the dish, then press around the edges to seal. Brush the surface with the reserved cream. Place the dishes on a metal tray and bake for 20–25 minutes, or until the pastry is golden. Serve with a crisp green salad.

1

2

3

PORK LOIN ROAST WITH APPLE WALNUT STUFFING AND ROAST VEGETABLES

Preparation time: 15 minutes + 10 minutes standing
Cooking time: 1 hour 30 minutes
Serves 4

50 g (1¾ oz/½ cup) walnuts, chopped
1 green apple, peeled and cored
½ teaspoon ground cinnamon
2 tablespoons port
1.5 kg (3 lb 5 oz) rindless, boned pork loin
100 ml (3½ fl oz) maple syrup
8 parsnips, sliced thinly lengthways
500 g (1 lb 2 oz) baby carrots
2 tablespoons oil

Preheat the oven to moderately hot 200°C (400°F/Gas 6). Grease a large roasting tin. Spread the walnuts on a baking tray and place under a medium–high grill (broiler) for 2–3 minutes, or until lightly toasted.

1 Coarsely grate the apple and squeeze out the excess juice. Combine the apple, cinnamon, walnuts and port and season to taste.
2 Unroll the pork loin, then spread the stuffing evenly over one third of the loin lengthways. Re-roll the loin, tie securely and place, seam-side-down, in the prepared tin. Roast for 20 minutes. Reduce the heat to moderate 180°C (350°F/Gas 4), baste the pork with some maple syrup and roast for a further 30 minutes.
3 Toss together the parsnip, carrots and oil in a large bowl and season if necessary. Add to the roasting tin and roast for a further 30–35 minutes, or until the vegetables are golden and tender. In the last 10 minutes of cooking, baste the pork again with the syrup. Remove the roast pork from the tin, cover with foil and allow to rest for 10 minutes before slicing. Serve with the vegetables and any pan juices.

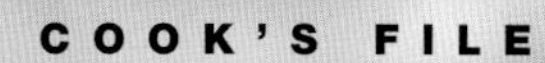

COOK'S FILE

Variation: If you don't have port on hand, use 2 tablespoons apple cider.

1

2

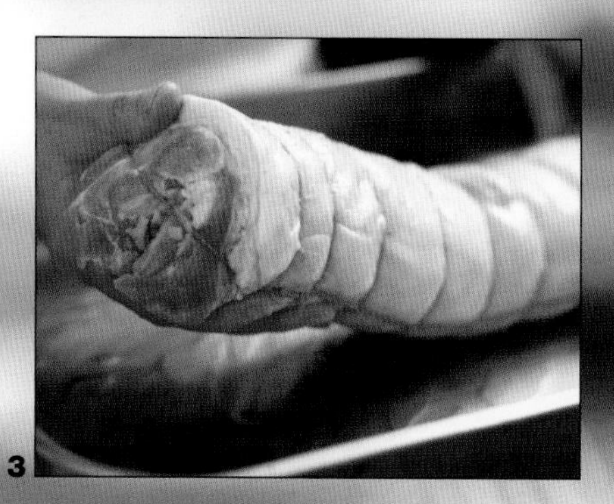
3

MUSHROOM AND TOMATO TARTS

Preparation time: 10 minutes
Total cooking time: 22 minutes
Serves 4

- 1 sheet ready-rolled puff pastry
- 2 tablespoons soft cream cheese
- 2 tablespoons oil
- 100 g (3½ oz) button mushrooms, sliced
- 2 cloves garlic, crushed
- ½ teaspoon dried mixed herbs
- 4 cherry tomatoes, sliced
- 1 tablespoon grated Parmesan cheese

1 Preheat oven to 240°C (475°F/ Gas 9). Brush an oven tray with melted butter or oil. Cut pastry into quarters. Place on tray. Fold edges over to form a 1 cm (½ inch) border, press down firmly. Spread cream cheese over pastry.

2 Heat oil in pan, add mushrooms, garlic and herbs. Stir over medium heat for 2 minutes or until softened and lightly golden; drain on paper towels. Arrange mushroom mixture over cream cheese, top with tomato, sprinkle with cheese. Bake 20 minutes or until pastry is puffed and golden.

COOK'S FILE

Note: Drain vegetables well before arranging over cream cheese.

1

2

TWO-POTATO GRATIN

Preparation time: 15 minutes
Total cooking time: 45 minutes
Serves 4

4 small potatoes
1 large orange sweet potato
1 small onion, thinly sliced
125 ml (4 fl oz/½ cup) chicken stock
65 g (2¼ oz/½ cup) finely grated Gruyère cheese

1 Preheat oven to 180°C (350°F/ Gas 4). Grease a shallow 2-litre (4 cup) ovenproof dish.
2 Peel potatoes and sweet potato and cut into slices. Place potato and onion in prepared dish in alternating layers. Pour chicken stock over potato, sprinkle evenly with cheese and bake for 45 minutes, or until golden brown.

1

Desserts

LATE CHERRY PARFAIT

eam (1–2 scoops each)
pitted black cherries, drained
lamington or choc-chip flavoured ice cream (1–2 scoops each)
4 tablespoons good-quality chocolate sauce
dark chocolate cherry bar, chopped, to garnish

Divide the chocolate ice cream, cherries and lamington ice cream among four parfait glasses. Drizzle with the chocolate sauce and garnish with the chocolate cherry bar. Serve at once. Serves 4.

BANANA CARAMEL ICE CREAM STACK

400 g (14 oz) pound cake, cut into 1.5 cm (5/8 inch) thick slices (you will need eight slices)
4 rectangular slabs vanilla ice cream
2 large bananas, cut on the diagonal into 1 cm (1/2 inch) slices
3 tablespoons good-quality caramel sauce, plus extra to drizzle
4 tablespoons honey-roasted macadamia nuts, chopped, plus extra, to garnish

Place a slice of cake on each of four serving plates, then top each slice with an ice cream slab. Divide the banana slices, caramel sauce and chopped nuts among each serving, then top with another slice of cake. Drizzle with extra caramel sauce and scatter with the extra nuts. Serve immediately. Serves 4.

INDIVIDUAL MANGO PASSIONFRUIT TRIFLES

60 g (2¼ oz) plain sponge cake, cut into 1 cm (½ inch) pieces
2 tablespoons Cointreau
2 small or 1 large mango, cut into bite-sized slices
2 tablespoons passionfruit pulp
125 ml (4 fl oz/½ cup) ready-made vanilla custard
200 g (7 oz) mascarpone
1 tablespoon icing (confectioner's) sugar
passionfruit pulp, extra, to garnish (optional)

Divide the cake pieces among four tall glasses. Drizzle 2 teaspoons Cointreau over the cake in each glass, then leave for 5 minutes. Arrange half the mango on the cake. Divide the passionfruit pulp and custard evenly among the glasses, then top with the remaining mango slices. Gently combine the mascarpone and icing sugar until light and creamy. Just before serving, dollop the mascarpone mixture on top and garnish with extra passionfruit. Serve at once. Serves 4.

Note: Another 1–2 tablespoons of custard can replace the layer of mascarpone, if preferred.

MELON WITH LEMONGRASS SYRUP

3 tablespoons caster (superfine) sugar
3 fresh makrut (kaffir lime) leaves
2 lemongrass stems (white part only), bruised
2 thin slices fresh ginger
250 g (9 oz) watermelon, deseeded and peeled
250 g (9 oz) honeydew melon
250 g (9 oz) rockmelon
12 lychees, peeled

Heat the sugar and 250 ml (9 fl oz/1 cup) water in a small saucepan over medium heat and stir until the sugar has dissolved. Add the lime leaves, lemongrass and ginger, and simmer rapidly for 5–7 minutes, or until thickened. Cool completely. Cut each melon into 2 cm (¾ inch) cubes, then place in a large bowl with the lychees. Discard the lime leaves, lemongrass and ginger from the syrup. Pour the syrup over the fruit and serve with vanilla ice cream, if desired. Serves 4.

Hint: The longer the fruit sits in the syrup, the better-the flavours will develop as the fruit becomes infused with the syrup. It will store well for up to 3 days in the refrigerator.

LIME DELICIOUS PUDDING

60 g (2¼ oz) butter, softened
4 tablespoons caster (superfine) sugar
3 eggs, separated
1½ teaspoons finely grated lime zest
3 tablespoons self-raising flour
185 ml (6 fl oz/¾ cup) milk
3 tablespoons lime juice
icing (confectioner's) sugar, to dust

Preheat the oven to 180°C (350°F/Gas 4) and lightly grease four 250 ml (9 fl oz/1 cup) ramekins. Beat the butter, sugar, egg yolks and lime zest with electric beaters until light and creamy. Fold the flour into the mixture in two batches, alternating with the milk and lime juice. Beat the egg whites in a clean, dry bowl, until just stiff, then lightly fold into the pudding mixture until just combined. Spoon into the prepared ramekins and place into a large, deep baking tray. Pour in enough water to come halfway up the side of the ramekins and bake for 25 minutes, or until risen and golden on top. Dust lightly with icing sugar and serve at once. Serves 4.

CHOCOLATE CROISSANT PUDDING

3 eggs
3 tablespoons caster (superfine) sugar
310 ml (10¾ oz/1¼ cups) milk
3 plain croissants, torn into small pieces
100 g (3½ oz) rum and raisin dark chocolate, roughly chopped
1 tablespoon mixed peel
1 tablespoon demerara sugar

Preheat the oven to 180°C (350°F/Gas 4). Grease a 1.25 litre (5 cup) rectangular ovenproof dish. In a separate bowl, whisk the eggs and sugar together until the sugar dissolves, then whisk in the milk until combined and frothy. Place half the croissants in the prepared dish, scatter the chocolate and mixed peel on top, then pour on half the egg mixture. Repeat with the remaining croissant pieces and egg mixture. Sprinkle the surface with the demerara sugar. Place the dish in a large deep baking tray. Pour in enough water to come halfway up the sides of the dish and bake for 40–45 minutes, or until set and golden on top. Serve with ice cream. Serves 4–6.

APPLE CRUMBLE

6 apples, peeled, cored and finely sliced
2 cinnamon sticks
2 cm x 4 cm (¾ inch x 1½ inch) piece lemon zest
4 tablespoons soft brown sugar
50 g (1¾ oz) chopped unsalted butter
60 g (2¼ oz/½ cup) plain (all-purpose) flour
2 tablespoons flaked almonds

Preheat the oven to 200°C (400°F/Gas 6). Lightly grease a 1.25 litre (5 cup) ovenproof dish. Place the apple, cinnamon sticks, lemon zest, 1 tablespoon of the brown sugar, and 125 ml (4 fl oz/½ cup) water in a large saucepan. Simmer, partially covered, over medium heat for 8–10 minutes, or until the apple is tender but still holding its shape. Discard the cinnamon and lemon rind. Transfer the apple mixture to the prepared dish. Mix the plain flour, 40 g (1½ oz) of the butter and 2 tablespoons of the brown sugar in a small bowl with your fingertips, rubbing in the butter until it resembles coarse breadcrumbs. Mix in the almonds until well coated. Sprinkle the crumble mixture over the apples, then scatter the remaining butter and soft brown sugar on top. Bake for 15 minutes, or until golden brown. Serve hot or cold, with custard or ice cream. Serves 4.

CHERRY GALETTES

2 sheets ready-rolled puff pastry
200 g (7 oz) cream cheese, softened
1 tablespoon grated lemon zest
670 g (1 lb 7 oz) jar morello cherries, drained
3 tablespoons sour cherry jam, melted
thick (double/heavy) cream, to serve

Preheat the oven to 200°C (400°F/Gas 6). Cut two rounds, 14 cm (5½ inch) diameter, from each sheet of pastry. Prick each round several times with a fork and place on a large baking tray. Bake for 5 minutes, then cool slightly. Mix the cream cheese and lemon rind together, then divide among the pastry rounds, spreading to leave a 2 cm (¾ inch) border around the edge of the pastry. Arrange about 4 tablespoons cherries on each round, and brush the surface with the melted jam. Bake for 20 minutes, or until the pastry is puffed and golden. Serve hot with a dollop of thick cream. Serves 4.

BELLINI SORBET

Preparation time: 20 minutes + freezing
Total cooking time: 2 minutes
Serves 6

500 g (1 lb 2 oz/2 cups) caster (superfine) sugar
5 large peaches
185 ml (6 fl oz/¾ cup) Champagne
2 egg whites

1 Combine sugar and 1 litre (4 cups) water in large pan. Stir over medium heat without boiling until sugar has dissolved. Bring to the boil, add peaches and simmer for 20 minutes. Remove peaches from pan with a slotted spoon and cool completely. Reserve 250 ml (9 fl oz/1 cup) of the poaching liquid.
2 Peel skin from the peaches. Remove stones and cut flesh into chunks. Place in food processor and process until smooth. Add reserved liquid and Champagne and process briefly until combined.
3 Pour mixture into a shallow metal tray and freeze until just firm—about 6 hours. Transfer mixture to a large mixing bowl. Using electric beaters, beat until smooth.
4 Beat egg whites until soft peaks form. Using a metal spoon, gently fold beaten egg white into sorbet mixture. Return to metal tray and freeze until firm. Serve sorbet in scoops, with sliced fresh peaches and dessert wafers, if desired.

COOK'S FILE

Storage time: Sorbet may be made up to 2 days in advance; cover tightly.
Hint: To make sorbet in an ice-cream churn, pour mixture into machine after adding Champagne and churn until beginning to freeze. Add beaten egg white, continue churning until ready. It will be slow to freeze due to the amount of alcohol and sugar.
Variation: Other soft stone fruits, such as nectarines or plums, can be used to make sorbet if you prefer.

1

2

3

4

APRICOT AND MACADAMIA NUT ICE-CREAM

Preparation time: 10 minutes
Total cooking time: nil
Serves 4

500 ml (17 fl oz/2 cups) vanilla ice-cream, softened slightly
70 g (2½ oz/½ cup) chopped, roasted, unsalted macadamia nuts
3 tablespoons chopped plain, sweet biscuits
3 tablespoons glacé apricots, chopped

1 Place all ingredients in a medium bowl. Stir until combined. Spoon mixture into 4 serving glasses, freeze until firm.

COOK'S FILE

Storage time: This recipe can be made a day ahead. Store in freezer.
Variation: Add 2 tablespoons of Grand Marnier.

1

PEARS IN RED WINE

Preparation time: 20 minutes
Total cooking time: 55 minutes
Serves 4

4 firm pears
750 ml (26 fl oz/3 cups) good-quality red wine
185 g (6½ oz/¾ cup) caster (superfine) sugar
1 cinnamon stick
3 tablespoons orange juice
5 cm (2 inch) piece orange zest
200 g (7 oz) mascarpone cheese

1 Peel pears, being careful to keep them whole with stalks attached.

2 Place wine, sugar, cinnamon stick, orange juice and zest in a large pan. Stir over heat until sugar is dissolved; add cinnamon and zest. Add pears, stir gently to coat. Cover pan; simmer for 20–25 minutes or until pears are cooked. Allow to cool in syrup.

3 Remove pears and drain on paper towels. Bring liquid to boil and boil rapidly without lid until only 185 ml (6 fl oz/¾ cup) liquid remains. Serve pears with a little syrup and mascarpone.

COOK'S FILE

Storage time: Pears may be cooked several hours ahead.

1

2

FRUIT MEDLEY BREAD PUDDING

Preparation time: 15 minutes
Total cooking time: 1 hour
Serves 4

5 slices, white bread
30 g (1 oz) butter
140 g(5 oz/¾ cup) dried fruit medley
4 eggs
625 ml (21½ fl oz/2½ cups) milk
4 tablespoons caster (superfine) sugar
½ teaspoon ground cinnamon

1 Preheat oven to 160°C (315°F/Gas 2–3). Remove crusts from bread and spread bread with butter. Cut slices diagonally in half. Place half the bread, buttered-side-up, in a 1.5 litre (6 cup) ovenproof dish. Top with the fruit medley and remaining bread, buttered-side-up.

2 Whisk eggs, milk and sugar in a large jug until combined. Pour over bread. Sprinkle with cinnamon. Place dish in a shallow baking dish. Pour in enough hot water to come halfway up the sides. Bake 1 hour or until set and lightly golden. Remove dish from water immediately.

COOK'S FILE

Storage time: Serve warm or at room temperature. If serving at room temperature, cook several hours ahead.

1

2

CHERRY CLAFOUTIS

Preparation time: 15 minutes
Total cooking time: 40 minutes
Serves 6–8

500 g (1 lb 2 oz) fresh cherries, or 800 g (1 lb 12 oz) tin pitted cherries, well drained
60 g (2¼ oz/½ cup) self-raising flour
4 tablespoons sugar
2 eggs, lightly beaten
250 ml (9 fl oz/1 cup) milk
25 g (¾ oz) butter, melted
icing (confectioner's) sugar, for dusting

1 Preheat oven to 180°C (350°F/Gas 4). Brush a 23 cm (9 inch) glass or ceramic shallow pie plate with melted butter. Pit the cherries and spread into the dish in a single layer. If using canned cherries, drain them well before placing in the dish.
2 Sift the flour into a medium bowl, add sugar and make a well in the centre. Add combined eggs, milk and butter gradually, whisking until just combined; do not over-beat.
3 Pour the batter over the cherries and bake for 40 minutes. Remove from oven and dust generously with icing sugar. Serve immediately.

COOK'S FILE

Storage time: Clafoutis is best made just before serving.
Hint: If using tinned cherries, make sure you drain them well or the finished dish will be very soggy.
Variation: Other berries—blueberries, blackberries, raspberries, or small, well flavoured strawberries—may be used instead if you prefer. A delicious version can be made using slices of poached pear.

1

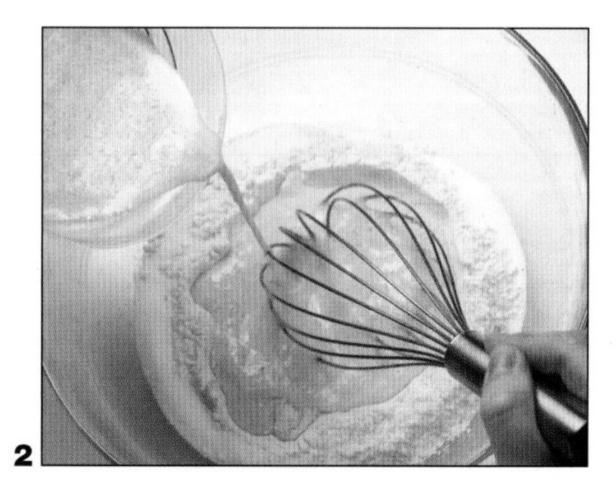

2

3

MANGO MILLE FEUILLE

Preparation time: 10 minutes
Total cooking time: 10 minutes
Serves 8

1 sheet ready rolled puff pastry
20 g (¾ oz) butter, melted
2 teaspoons cinnamon sugar

Filling
125 g (4½ oz) cream cheese
2 tablespoons caster (superfine) sugar
125 g (4½ oz/½ cup) sour cream
1 teaspoon vanilla extract
2 mangoes, peeled, sliced
icing (confectioner's) sugar, for dusting

1 Preheat oven to 200°C (400°F/ Gas 6). Line an oven tray with baking paper. Cut pastry into eight 6 cm x 12 cm (2½ inch x 4½ inch) rectangles. Place pastry onto prepared oven trays. Brush with a little butter, sprinkle with cinnamon sugar. Bake in preheated oven for 8–10 minutes, or until puffed and golden; cool.

2 Using electric beaters, beat the cream cheese and sugar in a small bowl until smooth. Add sour cream and extract and beat until smooth and thick.

3 Cut each pastry in half horizontally. Spoon or pipe some cheese mixture onto each pastry base, top with mango slices, then pastry tops. Dust tops with sifted icing sugar.

1

2

3

1

2

BAKED CUSTARD

Preparation time: 5 minutes
Total cooking time: 35 minutes
Serves 4

3 eggs
95 g (3¼ oz/½ cup) soft brown sugar
375 ml (13 fl oz/1½ cups) milk
125 ml (4 fl oz/½ cup) cream
1 teaspoon vanilla extract
ground nutmeg, for dusting

1 Preheat oven to 180°C (350°F/Gas 4). Brush a 1 litre (4 cup) capacity ovenproof dish with melted butter. Whisk eggs, sugar, milk, cream and vanilla in medium bowl for 1 minute. Pour into prepared dish.

2 Place filled dish into a shallow baking dish. Pour enough hot water into baking dish to come halfway up the sides. Place on oven shelf, sprinkle top of custard with nutmeg; bake for 15 minutes. Reduce heat to 160°C (315°F/Gas 2–3), bake for another 20 minutes or until custard is set and a sharp knife comes out clean when inserted. Remove dish from water immediately. Serve warm or cold.

COOK'S FILE

Storage time: Mixture can be prepared several hours ahead. If serving warm, cook just before serving. If serving cold, custard can be cooked a day in advance. Store, covered, in refrigerator.

1

2

APPLE PUFF SQUARES

Preparation time: 15 minutes
Total cooking time: 15 minutes
Serves 4

1 sheet ready-rolled puff pastry
60 g (2¼ oz) butter, melted
2 tablespoons soft brown sugar
½ teaspoon ground mixed spice
2 medium Granny Smith apples

1 Preheat oven to 210°C (415°F/Gas 6–7). Cut pastry into 4 squares, place on an oven tray. Combine butter, sugar and spice, brush half the mixture over pastry squares.
2 Peel apples, cut into wedges, remove core. Cut apple into very thin slices, lay on top of pastry squares leaving a 1 cm (½ inch) border.
3 Brush squares with remaining butter mixture. Bake for 15 minutes or until apple is tender and lightly golden. Cut each in half for serving.

COOK'S FILE

Storage time: Cook this dish just before serving.

PEACHES AND CREAM TRIFLE

Preparation time: 20 minutes
Total cooking time: nil
Serves 6–8

825 g (1 lb 13 oz) tin sliced peaches
3 tablespoons marsala
1 day-old sponge cake, cut into cubes
250 ml (9 fl oz/1 cup) cream
220 g (7¾ oz/1 cup) mascarpone
3 tablespoons flaked almonds, toasted

1 Drain peaches, reserving 125 ml (4 fl oz/½ cup) juice. Combine marsala and reserved juice. Place sponge cake cubes in a 2-litre (8 cup) dish and press down firmly. Drizzle with Marsala mixture.

2 Arrange peaches over cake. Using electric beaters, beat cream until soft peaks form. Add mascarpone and beat until just combined. Spread mixture over peaches. Refrigerate for 1 hour to allow flavours to develop. Sprinkle with almonds just before serving.

APPLE BETTY

Preparation time: 15 minutes
Total cooking time: 25 minutes
Serves 6

2 x 410 g (14 oz) tins pie apple
5 slices fruit bread
40 g (1½ oz) soft butter
2 teaspoons cinnamon sugar

1 Preheat oven to 180°C (350°F/ Gas 4).

2 Spread apple over base of 1.5 litre (6 cup) ovenproof dish. Cut crusts from bread, spread both sides with butter. Sprinkle 1 side with cinnamon sugar. Cut into cubes and arrange bread in an even layer over apple. Bake for 25 minutes or until golden.

1

SELF-SAUCING BAKED CHOCOLATE PUDDING

Preparation time: 25 minutes
Total cooking time: 40 minutes
Serves 4–6

125 g (4½ oz/1 cup) self-raising flour
2 tablespoons cocoa powder
125 g (4½ oz/½ cup) caster (superfine) sugar
125 ml (4 fl oz/½ cup) milk
1 egg
60 g (2¼ oz) butter, melted
1 teaspoon vanilla extract
2 tablespoons cocoa powder, extra
185 g (6½ oz/¾ cup) caster (superfine) sugar, extra

1 Preheat oven to 180°C (350°F/Gas 4). Brush a 2 litre (8 cup) oven proof dish with melted butter or oil. Sift dry ingredients into a large mixing bowl; make a well in the centre.

2 Pour in combined milk, egg, butter and essence. Stir until smooth; do not over-beat. Pour into prepared dish.

3 Dissolve extra cocoa powder and sugar in 625 ml (21½ fl oz/2½ cups) boiling water. Pour gently over the back of a spoon onto the pudding mixture.

4 Bake for 40 minutes or until a skewer comes out clean when inserted. Top may be dusted with sifted icing (confectioner's) sugar.

COOK'S FILE

Hint: Serve with some of the sauce.

1

2

3

ORANGE BANANA CREPES

Preparation time: 15 minutes
Total cooking time: 15 minutes
Serves 4

85 g (3 oz/⅔ cup) self-raising flour
2 eggs
125 ml (4 fl oz/½ cup) milk
60 g (2¼ oz) butter
4 tablespoons soft brown sugar
3 teaspoons grated orange zest
3 tablespoons orange juice
3 bananas, sliced

1 Sift flour into a medium bowl; make a well in the centre. Whisk eggs, milk and 3 tablespoons water until combined. Add gradually to flour. Stir until the liquid is incorporated and batter is free of lumps. Pour 2–3 tablespoons of batter onto lightly greased 20 cm (8 inch) non-stick pan; swirl evenly over base. Cook over medium heat for 1 minute or until underside is golden. Turn crepe over; cook other side. Transfer to a plate; cover with a tea-towel, keep warm. Repeat process with remaining batter, greasing pan when necessary. You will need 8 crepes for this recipe.

2 Heat butter in medium pan, add sugar and stir over low heat until sugar is dissolved and mixture is bubbling. Add zest and juice. Bring to boil; reduce heat. Simmer, uncovered, for 2 minutes. Add banana; simmer for 1 minute. Divide mixture among the 8 crepes. Fold crepes into quarters to enclose. Place crepes on serving plates.

1

COOK'S FILE

Storage time: Batter can be made. several hours in advance. Leave, covered with plastic wrap. Cook crepes just before serving. Alternatively, crepes can be cooked several hours in advance. Place on a baking tray; cover with aluminium foil. Just before serving, place crepes in 180°C (350°F/ Gas 4) oven for 10 minutes or until warmed through.

2

SPICED BAKED APPLES

Preparation time: 20 minutes
Total cooking time: 45 minutes
Serves 4

4 medium Granny Smith apples
3 tablespoons raw sugar
3 tablespoons figs, chopped
3 tablespoons dried apricots, chopped
3 tablespoons slivered almonds
1 tablespoon apricot jam
¼ teaspoon ground cardamom
¼ teaspoon ground cinnamon
30 g (1 oz) butter

1 Preheat oven to 180°C (350°F/Gas 4). Brush a square, deep ovenproof dish with melted butter. Peel the apples and remove the cores. Gently roll each apple in sugar. In a medium bowl, combine figs, apricots, almonds, jam and spices.

2 Fill each apple with the fruit mixture. Place apples in prepared dish. Dot with pieces of butter.

3 Bake for 35–40 minutes or until apples are tender. Serve warm with cream or ice-cream.

COOK'S FILE

Storage time: Baked apples are best prepared and baked just before being served.

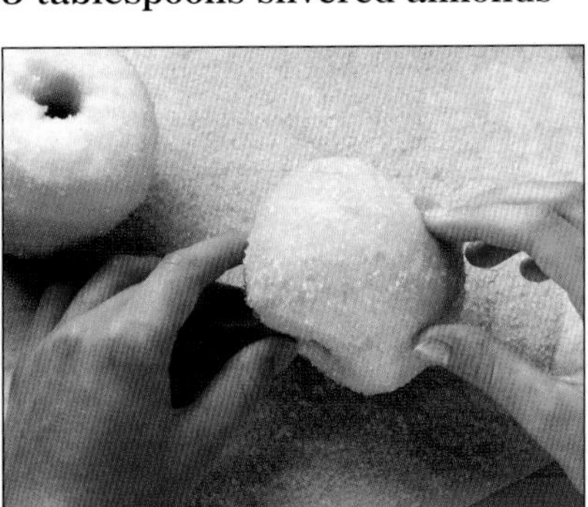

1

2

3

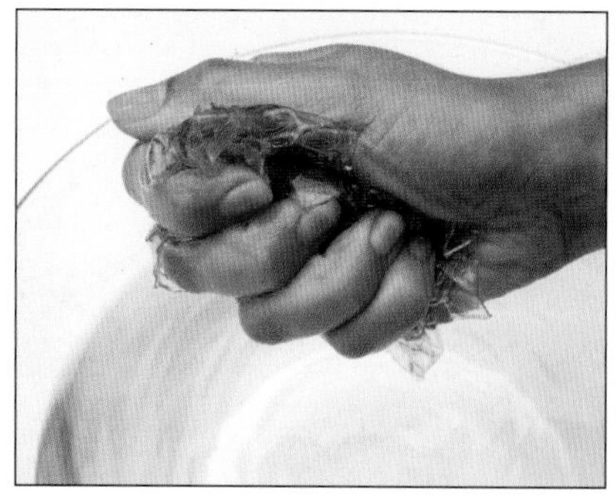

After soaking, squeeze the sheets of gelatine to remove any excess water.

Stir the gelatine sheets into the hot liquid until they have dissolved.

Divide the lychees among the wine glasses, gently dropping them into the jelly mixture.

GINGER AND LYCHEE JELLY

Preparation time: 10 minutes + 4 hours setting
Total cooking time: 5 minutes
Serves 6

565 g (1 lb 4 oz) tin lychees
500 ml (17 fl oz/2 cups) clear apple juice (no added sugar)
4 tablespoons strained lime juice
2 tablespoons caster (superfine) sugar
3 cm x 3 cm (1¼ inch x 1¼ inch) piece fresh ginger, peeled and thinly sliced
4 sheets gelatine (about 5 g or ⅛ oz)
mint to garnish

1 Drain the syrup from the lychees and reserving 250 ml (9 fl oz/1 cup) of the syrup. Discard the remaining syrup. Place reserved syrup, apple juice, lime juice, sugar and ginger in a saucepan. Bring to the boil, then reduce heat and simmer for 5 minutes. Strain into a heatproof bowl.

2 Place the gelatine sheets in a large bowl of cold water and soak for 2 minutes, or until they soften. Squeeze out the excess water, then add to the syrup. Stir until the gelatine has completely dissolved. Leave to cool.

3 Pour 2 tablespoons of the jelly mixture into each of six 150 ml (5 fl oz) stemmed wine glasses, and divide the lychees among the wine glasses. Refrigerate until the jelly has set. Spoon the remaining jelly over the fruit and refrigerate until set. Before serving, garnish with mint leaves.

COOK'S FILE

Note: Sprinkle 1 tablespoon slivered almonds among the jelly, if desired.

1

2

3

BANANA FRITTERS WITH CARAMEL SAUCE

Preparation time: 10 minutes
Total cooking time: 10 minutes
Serves 4

125 g (4½ oz/1 cup) self-raising flour
1 egg, beaten
185 ml (6 fl oz/¾ cup) soda water
oil, for deep-frying
4 bananas, each cut into quarters
ice-cream, for serving

Caramel sauce
185 g (6½ oz/1 cup) soft brown sugar
125 ml (4 fl oz/½ cup) cream
100 g (3½ oz) butter, chopped

1 Sift flour into medium bowl; make a well in the centre. Add egg and soda water all at once. Stir until all liquid is incorporated and batter is free of lumps.
2 Heat oil in heavy-based pan. Dip bananas in batter a few pieces at a time; drain off excess batter. Gently lower bananas into moderately hot oil. Cook over medium–high heat for 2 minutes or until golden, crisp and warmed through. Carefully remove from oil with a slotted spoon. Drain on paper towels; keep warm. Repeat with remaining bananas. Serve fritters immediately with ice cream and caramel sauce.
3 To make caramel sauce, combine all ingredients in a small pan and stir until sugar has dissolved and butter has melted. Bring to the boil; reduce heat and simmer for 2 minutes.

COOK'S FILE

Storage time: Bananas fritters are best cooked just before serving.
Hint: To prevent discolouration of bananas, don't cut them until you are ready to use them.
Variations: Serve banana fritters with chocolate, strawberry or mocha sauce or drizzle with honey.

QUICK PAVLOVAS

Preparation time: 15 minutes
Total cooking time: nil
Serves 6

300 g (10¼ oz) packet frozen raspberries
310 ml (10¾ fl oz/1¼ cups) cream
18 small meringues
2 flaky chocolate bars, roughly broken

1 Thaw raspberries according to directions on the packet. Using electric beaters, whip cream until soft peaks form. Fold raspberries through cream until just combined. Arrange meringues on serving plates. Spread cream mixture over and sprinkle with chocolate shards.

COOK'S FILE

Variation: Use chopped, fresh strawberries or drained canned fruit.

1

HOT PASSIONFRUIT SOUFFLE

Preparation time: 15 minutes
Total cooking time: 20–25 minutes
Serves 4–6

2 egg yolks
125 ml (4 fl oz/½ cup) passionfruit pulp (about 6 passionfruit)
2 tablespoons lemon juice
90 g (3¼ oz/¾ cup) icing (confectioner's) sugar
6 egg whites
icing (confectioner's) sugar, for decorating

1 Preheat oven to 210°C (425°F/ Gas 6–7). Lightly brush 4 individual (1 cup capacity) ramekin dishes or 1 large soufflé dish with oil or melted butter. Sprinkle base and sides with caster (superfine) sugar. Place a collar of baking paper around dishes, secure with string; lightly grease paper.
2 Combine yolks, pulp, lemon juice and half the icing sugar in a large bowl. Whisk until well combined.
3 With electric beaters, beat egg whites in large bowl until soft peaks form. Gradually add remaining icing sugar, beating well after each addition.
4 Using a large metal spoon, fold white mixture, in batches, through passionfruit mixture. Spoon into dishes. Using a flat-bladed knife, cut through mixture in a circular motion 2 cm (¾ inch) from the edge. Place dish on large oven tray, bake 20–25 minutes or until soufflé is well-risen and cooked through. Cut collars from dishes and serve soufflé immediately, sprinkled with sifted icing sugar.

COOK'S FILE

Storage time: Serve hot soufflés immediately on removing from oven.

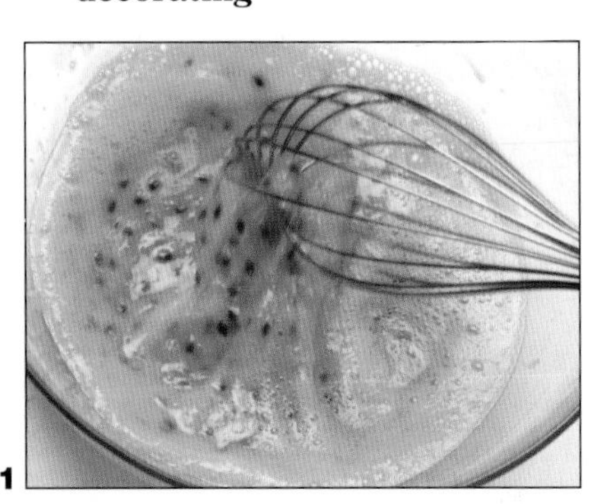

1

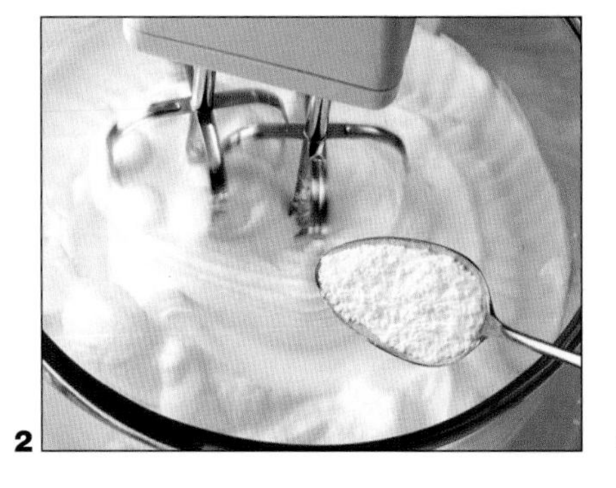

2

3

MACERATED FRUITS WITH MASCARPONE

Preparation time: 20 minutes
Total cooking time: 10 minutes
Serves 4–6

2 oranges
150 g (5½ oz/1 cup) raspberries
150 g (5½ oz/1 cup) blueberries
2 tablespoons caster (superfine) sugar
2 tablespoons sugar

1 Place each orange on a board and cut a 2 cm (¾ inch) wide slice from each end—cut down to where pulp starts.

2 Remove rind in wide strips, including all pith and white membrane. Using a small, sharp knife, cut pith from rind and discard; cut the rind into thin strips.

3 Separate orange segments by carefully cutting between membrane and flesh. Combine orange segments and berries in a medium bowl, sprinkle with caster sugar and toss lightly. Cover and refrigerate.

4 Combine 4 tablespoons water and sugar in a small pan and stir over low heat without boiling until the sugar has dissolved. Bring to the boil, reduce heat and add the orange rind. Simmer for 2 minutes until rind is tender; cool. Reserve 1 tablespoon of rind, combine syrup and remaining rind with berry mixture. Spoon into goblets and garnish with reserved rind; serve with large dollops of mascarpone.

1

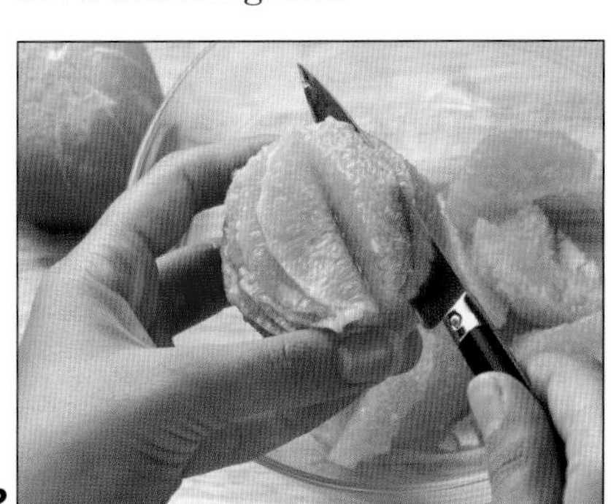
2

3

Index

Published in 2011 by Murdoch Books Pty Limited.

Murdoch Books Australia
Pier 8/9, 23 Hickson Road, Millers Point NSW 2000
Phone: +61 (0)2 8220 2000 Fax: +61 (0)2 8220 2558
www.murdochbooks.com.au

Murdoch Books UK Limited
Erico House, 6th Floor North, 93–99 Upper Richmond Road
Putney, London SW15 2TG
Phone: + 44 (0) 20 8785 5995 Fax: + 44 (0) 20 8785 5985
www.murdochbooks.co.uk

Publisher: Lynn Lewis
Senior Designer: Heather Menzies
Project Manager: Liz Malcolm
Designer: Kylie Mulquin
Editor: Justine Harding

ISBN: 978-0-68134-746-5

Printed by 1010 Printing International Limited. PRINTED IN CHINA.